We All Bleed Red

Insights and Perspectives from an Unidentifiable Visual Minority Man

Sensei Paul David

COPYRIGHT PAGE

We All Bleed Red: Insights and Perspectives from an Unidentifiable Visual Minority Man, by Sensei Paul David, Copyright © 2024

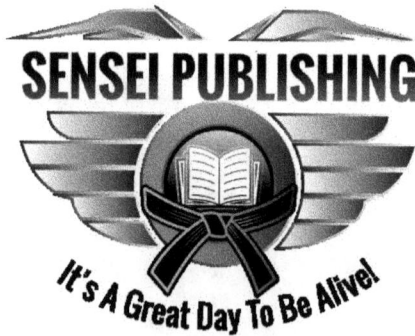

SENSEI PUBLISHING

It's A Great Day To Be Alive!

www.senseipublishing.com

@senseipublishing
#senseipublishing

Get/Share Your FREE SSD Mental Health Chronicles at
www.senseiselfdevelopment.care

or

CLICK HERE

Sensei Self Development

FOR ADULTS

An Introduction to Mindfulness

Sensei Paul David

Check Out The SSD Chronicles Series

CLICK HERE

Set As Browser Favorite

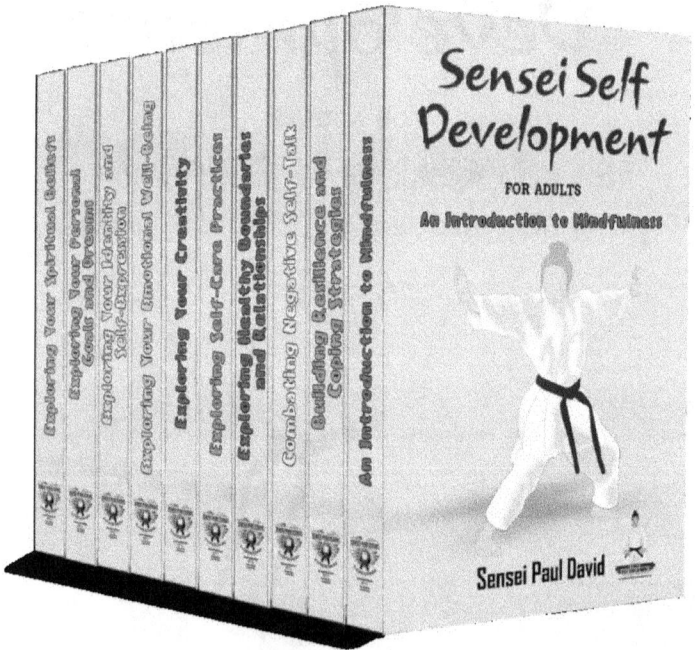

Get/Share Our FREE All-Ages Mental Health Books Now!

FREE Kids eBooks

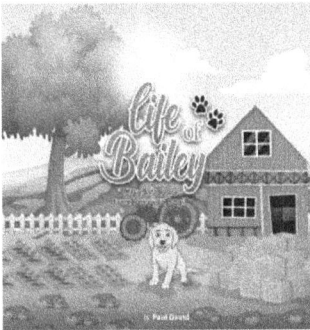

lifeofbailey.senseipublishing.com kidsonearth.senseipublishing.com

FREE Self-Development eBook for Every Family

senseiselfdevelopment.senseipublishing.com

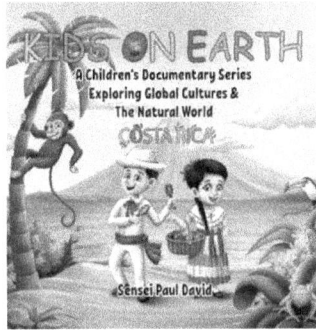

Click Below or Search Amazon for Another eBook In Each Series Or Visit:

www.senseipublishing.com/CompleteLibrary

KIDS ON EARTH

kidsonearth.senseipublishing.com

Life of Bailey

lifeofbailey.senseipublishing.com

SENSEI SELF DEVELOPMENT BOOKS SERIES

senseiselfdevelopment.senseipublishing.com

Dedication

To those who courageously take action towards self-improvement - you are helping to evolve the world for generations to come.

- It's a great day to be alive!

Get/Share Your FREE All-Ages Mental Health eBook Now at

www.senseiselfdevelopment.com

Or CLICK HERE

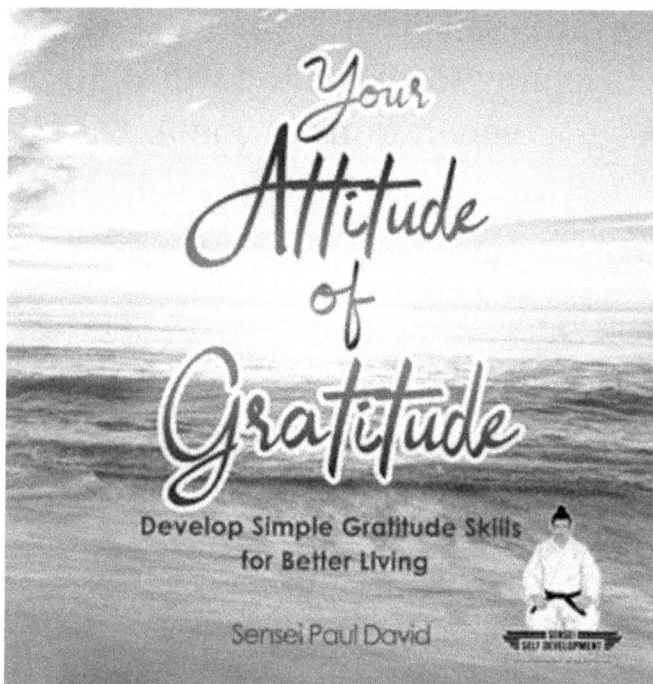

senseiselfdevelopment.com

Check Out Another Book In The SSD BOOK SERIES:

senseipublishing.com/SSD_SERIES

CLICK HERE

senseiselfdevelopment.senseipublishing.com

Join Our Publishing Journey!

If you would like to receive FUTURE FREE BOOKS and get to know us better, please click www.senseipublishing.com and join our newsletter by entering your email address in the pop-up box.

Follow Our Blog: senseipauldavid.ca

Follow/Like/Subscribe: Facebook, Instagram, YouTube: @senseipublishing

Scan the QR Code with your phone or tablet

to follow us on social media: Like / Subscribe / Follow

A Message From The Author:
Sensei Paul David

Dear Reader,

Welcome to a different world of mental health – a sacred space for self-reflection, growth, and healing. Within these pages, you hold the power to uplift your spirit, invigorate your mind, and challenge your preconceptions.

In a world that often moves at blink-and-you'll-miss-it speed, making time for intellectual discovery is crucial.

Together, we will navigate the labyrinth of emotions, and experiences.

This book is your compassionate companion, offering solace and understanding during your unique journey. Here, you are free to unburden yourself, and confront the challenges that may still linger.

Within the sheltered realm of these pages, there is no judgment, no expectation, and no pressure. Your unique experience and perspective hold immeasurable worth, and your voice deserves to be heard.

In this sacred space, you are challenged to take off the mask we so often wear in the outside world. It is here that you can be raw, vulnerable, and authentic – allowing your true self to be seen and embraced without reservation. By giving yourself permission to explore the depths of your emotions and confront the shadows that may lurk within, you will discover profound insights and find the insight you seek over time.

As you embark on this journey, I encourage you to embrace the process itself rather than fixate solely on the outcome. Remember, it is not about reaching a certain destination or ticking off boxes on a list of accomplishments. Rather, it is about cultivating self-awareness, fostering self-compassion, and nurturing a sense of curiosity about the intricate workings of your intelligently beautiful mind on this subject.

I am honored to be a part of your journey, and I believe in your ability to navigate the twists and turns with grace and resilience. Remember, you are not alone in this – countless others have walked similar paths, faced similar challenges, and emerged stronger and wiser on the other side.

With great respect for your decision to learn,

Paul David

TABLE OF CONTENTS

FOREWORD

Many assume that things will improve over time without the willingness to offer solutions to the current challenges. The truth is that time does not automatically sort things out. It is the effort of people over a period of time that changes situations. Racism has been a serious problem causing pain and anger to the victims. Sadly, due to its almost invisible nature in the modern world, it is easy for many people to assume that it does not exist.

Even when people believe that it exists, they usually don't feel that it is a serious problem. Many tend to downplay the seriousness of this issue and this is one of the reasons nothing substantial has been done to curb it.

In *We All Bleed Red*, Paul skillfully highlights the factors that perpetuate racism and its almost invisible nature in the modern world. This project is a perfect combination of personal experience and research to establish the reasons it is almost easy for some to overlook racism in the 21st century, the problems of racism, and plausible solutions to the problem.

Unlike many books out there, Paul didn't write like an activist trying to pour out his grievances through a book. Rather, he wrote like an observer trying to take his audience on a journey that will give them reasons to take racism more seriously. So, you can be sure that this is not one of those books where the author is trying to vent his frustration on the readers. Feel free to read and reason along. You will find reasons to want to be a part of the solution to racism after completing this compilation of history, experience, and research on racism.

INTRODUCTION

Opening Metaphor

Imagine this with me: Imagine yourself as a child who has lived in an underground soundproof room from birth. You've had some virtual access to the world's experiences and the world's knowledge and basic biological resources. You are educated and physically and emotionally normal. The only catch is, in this story, you've never been outside before, never actually heard, or seen, or experienced the outside world first-hand. All you know is the confines of this safe and predictable soundproof room, and so this experience of your life has been the norm for you.

Let's pretend you're not bothered by this strange concept (and why would you be if this is normal and real to you? Who's to say this is abnormal at all?). Therefore, you're not troubled by this way of life because there's nothing outside this room to compare your experience to. So, there's no logical reason for any discomfort.

Now, imagine I came to visit you one day. I sat you down, and I told you there was a powerful force out there called "wind," energy caused by the fluctuations of surface pressure atmosphere that is so strong at times it could dismantle a house from its foundation or reach potential speeds of approximately 300 miles per hour, (nearly half the speed of sound), or destroy the lives of communities, especially places around the world, with little to no warning.

Now, what if I said to you that you cannot see the wind and because you live in a soundproof room, you cannot hear the wind, you cannot feel it, and you cannot predict or accurately measure it, but trust me, the wind does exist! Would you have any logical reason to believe me? Probably not.

But let's say you wanted to believe me, but you had no reason to. So, you ask me to prove to you the wind exists, but you are either unable or unwilling to leave your soundproof room. Instead, you asked me to bring you a sample from the outside world. And I reply - I can't bring you a sample of wind because the nature of wind can only be felt but cannot be experienced if you stay in this room. How would you react to me then? Would you laugh? Would you ask me to leave? Would you ignore me? After all, if you can't measure or process something with your senses, how could it exist, right? How could it be real? And by that logic, maybe you'd think to yourself: if it doesn't affect me, why would I be curious or engaged? Why would I care? Of course, in the real world, we know better, but as a tribe of Canadians and Americans, do we?

Now let's pretend racism represents the wind and the child no longer represents you but represents the social norm, and the soundproof room represents cultural ignorance. No doubt, by now, you probably know where I'm going with this: racism is powerful, racism is invisible, and racism does not affect everyone equally. So, let's begin to break down this pattern together...

————————

PROLOGUE

To those who are new to the concept of the invisibility of racism:

This book presents a worthy and challenging opportunity to the mind. That is, to extend and evolve our peaceful perceptions of cultural discovery beyond social norms, racial ignorance, and most importantly, beyond what you thought you knew about the historic and subtle modern-day nature of racism in Canada and the United States. This book will also explore historic racism in the UK.

This book will not be easy to read for everyone. At times, it won't feel good, but if you stick with it, I genuinely believe it contains insights and perceptions everyone needs to hear with open-minded empathy.

PLEASE NOTE: If you visually present as White, the voice of this book may surprise you and cause you to self-reflect in a way that makes you feel uncomfortable - and I believe that's a good thing to help socially evolve your understanding of the baked-in propensities of racism affecting Visual Minority people (Black, Indigenous, People of Color) also known in the UK as BAME people (Black, Asian, and Minority Ethnic) and UVM people (Unidentifiable Visual Minority).

If you do NOT visually present as White, you may find reflections in this book that inspire questions about many of the untold histories of racism (that may go beyond this book), and you may also be able to relate to some of my personal stories and the stories of other Visual Minority people.

To you my intelligent and curious reader:

I don't know you, but I want you to know that I respect you for picking up this book, not because you're a 'valuable customer' helping to make me money or following me on social media but because reading this book proves that you've realized there's something wrong in the world. However, you cannot easily and specifically articulate its sources, nature, what to do about it, or how to go about it. You may feel like you want to do something but do not know what. You may want to learn and perceive more. You may not know what I mean at all but my point is, now that you've taken action by reading these words, it means everything to me, and this is why I respect you.

Furthermore, picking up this book means that you are willing to challenge what you may have been taught, have or have not experienced, have been ignorant of, or maybe reminded of your battle-hardened traumas, all due to the disease of racism. I believe that educational evolution of this kind, through dialogue and awareness, is highly defensive for some and uncomfortable for others. It's uncertain for many, unspoken for almost everyone, and ignored by far too many.

Let me be clear and honest with you because I care about your experience as you consume the information in this book: If you are attempting to not only agree with the existence of racism but also actually understand racism (and yes, there is a difference), attempting to understand the pain of racism can only be done through feeling the pain of it, and therefore not everyone will fully understand racist oppression.

You may agree or disagree, but many of you will not viscerally understand - and I want you to know that's okay and that this book is a safe place for you to think and perceive in ways you've never been encouraged to process before. As you read on, I encourage you to think with more than just your mind; I encourage you to think with your imagination and curiosity. Think with your instinct to connect with other human beings and to evolve by widening your observations of a lack of cultural diversity and cultural equality, to expose it and talk about it more and more, with people who both look like you and who don't look like you.

I don't pretend to know everything about racism myself, but my unique ethnicities and cultural '180-degree opposite' family dynamics (which I will share with you later), have given me a deep understanding of this topic from having grown up living as both a Visual Minority person and a visual majority (notice I said 'living,' not 'treated').

Similar to previous times, it's obvious you're here because you care and are curious, but more importantly, something about this topic is drawing you in to learn and experience more. Something has caused you to realize there is perpetual and invisible racism in the world, and you don't want to accidentally be part of the problem or unconsciously remain part of the problem. Instead, you want to be part of the solution - and yes, there is a direction leading to something resembling a solution.

If this sounds like you, you are in the right place. I can't guarantee this will be an easy journey for you to relate to, but I respect you for taking this journey with me. So, thanks in advance to my White brothers and sisters for all the mental effort you will put into the attempt to challenge past limiting and blinding social norms, to reach a form of independent thinking you may not have had before on this subject. And to my BIPOC brothers and sisters, I hope you will be inspired to gather your related insights and perspectives and have more uncomfortable conversations with each other and your White brothers and White sisters as well.

Moreover, my perspective is unique because it's not about being Black or White or Jewish. For me, it's about being an unidentifiable visual minority, which I feel puts me into a category of struggle of my own. I obviously can't speak for every minority. I'd like to invite you to join me as I share my life with you in a way that hopefully causes you to lean in and learn about the politically correct faces of racism - and its ripple-effect that cannot be measured or directly understood by some White-presenting people or those who present as White-presenting people. Like some of the best-learned lessons, it can only be felt.   So, I hope you can feel what I'm sharing with you, as you read on.

This Book's Purpose:

To bring awareness to the subtleties of modern-day racism for the unique perspective of being an Unidentifiable Visual Minority.

———————————————

This book's intention:

To inspire peaceful cross-cultural dialogue, via sharing my perspectives, experience, and insights into the origins and nature of racism and to discuss solutions to the invisibility of inequity to the unspoken realities of inequity to my visual majority brothers and sisters around the world, in the hope that it will inspire open discussions about inequity and explore global cultures with genuine goodwill and genuine curiosity.

Note: The discomfort you will feel is necessary because anti-racial discomfort helps to foster learning, which is essential to take the next step forward. Depending on how open your mind is, you may be surprised, shocked, or feel guilty, or you may empathize in between these pages. There's no wrong way to feel. On the topic of racism, there is a definite difference between agreement and understanding, and if you're White, without feeling discomfort, I believe you can't fully make that shift into understanding until you feel enough pain from racism. Let's face it, when it comes to pain, you can't understand it, unless you feel it.

This is not an angry or a social justice book, though I admit I have been angry about living this topic at times (hopefully by the end of this book, the reasons for that anger can be understood, even if just slightly, by people who present as White).

Thankfully, I feel the world is ready now for this topic to be discussed openly and peacefully and to continue to have dialogue (now that the civil rights movement has been rebooted as Black Lives Matter). I'm here to do my small part to try and keep this state of open-mindedness open for as long as possible.

———————————————————

Let's start with me....

My basic background:

I have both a Black culture family and I have a White culture family. I am an Unidentifiable Visual Minority man with Austrian roots on my father's side and

Jamaican roots on my mother's side, and I'm Jewish. I say I'm 'unidentifiable' because my physical features are not very telling of any ethnicity. I don't look fully White, and I don't look fully Black but I know that society identifies me as a BIPOC. All through this book, I will refer to people like me as Unidentifiable Visual Minority (UVM).

The life of a UVM can be complicated because you are set apart from identifiable BIPOC, which makes you incapable of fully enjoying the social benefits of being easily identified as Black, White, or Asian. This makes it more challenging to overcome societal demands due to the distraction of some people that are unnecessarily focused on ethnic labeling.

As an infant, I was converted to Judaism and raised as a Jew by my White father on the weekends, while during the week, I was raised by my Visual Minority mother without any religious influence of any kind. My parents divorced when I was 3 and my childhood and adolescence (I felt) were about living two different cultural lives at the same time, where I felt I was Black during weekdays and I felt I was White on the weekends.

My Visual Minority family is one generation older than I am, with one younger half-sibling on my mother's side. My White family is two generations older than I am and comprises Germanic and Middle Eastern Jews with four older half-siblings on my father's side. I was a child of the 1980s in Toronto, Canada, with no one who remotely looked like I did. Back then, being biracial wasn't just rare, it was nonexistent in my mother's neighborhood, and also in my father's neighborhood.

Black Indigenous or People of Color (BIPOC) didn't see me as completely Black and were okay, but at the time I felt White-presenting people seemed more distracted by the appearance of my unique ethnicity than anything else. I couldn't put that feeling into words as a child and later, as an adolescent (something to get into later). I'm the oldest sibling on my mother's side, and the youngest sibling on my father's side, whereas my White father was old enough to be a Canadian-born child of the Second World War. However, I am 12 years older than my younger brother on my Black mother's side, and I had a hand in helping to raise my younger brother as a parental figure.

So, I'm very comfortable saying I understand the cultural perceptions of racism from the viewpoints of White-presenting people spanning multiple generations, and I understand the perceptions of racism from the viewpoint of Visual Minority people, with the added understanding of presenting as a BIPOC in Toronto (which is a city that may be regarded as culturally diverse, but - in my mind, is far from anti-racist and could be as racially ignorant as any other North American city).

I was a project manager working in the Canadian financial services space for a US bank until I was knocked unconscious by a truck while crossing the street on my bicycle. Surviving this event, changed the course of my life and has led me to publish mental health and educational books for adults and kids. I have a Jiu-Jitsu Black belt, having trained with the Toronto Police Athletic Association, where I later became a volunteer instructor to high school kids at a martial arts club, outside downtown Toronto.

I'm also a private pilot, flying small aircraft at the Toronto island airport for personal enjoyment. And finally, I'm a self-taught musician of more than 20 years who conducts an R&B wedding trio. However, through my bottomless curiosity and an endless need to learn new things, I've always been keenly aware of how the norms of society regard and treat my two families, as well as my unwillingness to talk about it to either family.

I noticed how the world seemed to take my White father so seriously whenever he complained, asked a question, or had a request. Wherever we went, I thought my father was so influential, solely because of who he was (a strong, scientifically intelligent force and motivated person). But I also noticed that my mother (as equally strong, motivated, and emotionally intelligent) was not taken as seriously as my father was by White-presenting people. My mother had to ingratiate herself to be heard and taken seriously, which took a lot longer and didn't work as well as my father's 'bend everything to your will' attitude to everything.

I admit, as a kid, I didn't have the vocabulary I have now to express myself on observing these differences in social acceptance, but deep down, I unconsciously decided not to say anything to my White family because I was afraid of not being understood or dismissed. I felt there was no point in trying to start a dialogue because no one would believe me due to a problem they didn't know existed and could not relate to and therefore could not understand. This was the result of the mental simulation I conjured over and over again.

I never said anything about my observations of inequity to my Visual Minority family because I didn't want to remind them or embarrass them about how unfair it was for me to see my Visual Minority family having to work much harder than my White family for far less opportunity, with far fewer resources. And while all of this was happening, I didn't see I was not only culturally confused, but I didn't know who I was, and I got used to feeling alone, in that I had no one to turn to for biracial guidance. No one suspected I was having a cultural and racial crisis, and I taught myself to be one of those people.

————————

Chapter One:
My Ethnic Colors

I battled identity crisis in my teenage years, and this was because I have a White-presenting father, but I present as a Visual Minority person. My connection with Judaism was also another aspect of my life that complicated things for me. It is as though I am in three groups where I am not fully accepted no matter how hard I try to adapt. In this chapter, I will share my dilemma with you, as we progress on this journey to racial enlightenment.

My Being White

My father was White, but I'm not taken nearly as seriously by White-presenting people as he was. This makes it difficult to be taken seriously or patiently when face to face with White-presenting people when I have a complaint, or a question, or during a job interview, etc. No one sees me as White, and therefore I'm not entitled to White privileges or social entitlements. In my early years, I thought my father is White and that should help me to enjoy certain social privileges, but it never materialized. I learned how to express my White culture, behavior, word choice, and humor, especially when around my White family.

That ethnic side of my family was very large, and I was, and still am, the only person of color in that family after three generations of observation. There are no biracial people in my White family. I tried to identify as being White to my White friends, but it is often awkward. My skin color stares them in the face while I claim to be White because of my father. I had to explain to everyone who cared to listen, that I am White, even though my skin is Black. After many failed attempts, I realized that the fact that my father is White wouldn't change anything about how people perceived me because of the color of my skin.

It started getting to me that no one was seeing me as a White person, and I decided that I should let my father know about it. However, it was never productive. He threw it out of the window and told me to focus on self-development rather than allowing myself to be distracted by issues regarding racism. I cannot blame him because he is a victim of the days of political correctness when it comes to racism. It is not obvious to him because he cannot experience it and has not observed what I call: Invisible Inequality.

He never said it, but I felt he would consider the opinion that Visual Minority people talk about racism when they are looking for an excuse for their failure. He agreed with the fact that it is wrong for people to treat others in a wrong way, based on the color of their skin. Still, he did not believe that such people make up the majority of society. He would often tell me that I shouldn't allow the opinion of some of the few dumb people to affect me. He would cite the examples of certain Visual Minority people that are prominent in various fields, to defend the fact that Visual Minority people can become whatever they want to become if they are willing to pay the price.

This logic and sentiment that my White father has are common in the UK, Canada, and the US today. It seems to be a sound argument because it is true that many Visual Minority people have been able to reach the pinnacle of their careers in different fields. Stellar names like Michael Jordan, Mike Tyson, Evander Holyfield, Dwayne Johnson, and Barack Obama come to mind to buttress this argument. However, a critical view of every one of these people will reveal to you that they are exceptions rather than the norm. In the case of Barack Obama, he remains the only Visual Minority American president the US has ever had.

Dwayne Johnson is the only Visual Minority in the list of top ten popular Hollywood actors of 2021. So, it is not that simple to dismiss the fact that Visual Minority people are marginalized and discriminated against, just because we have some Visual Minority people that were able to break the barriers and make a difference. No matter the situation, there will always be diamonds in the rough. There will always be that person or some people that were able to reach their goals in life, even though they faced unfavorable circumstances. That's the type of mindset I have. I don't want to make excuses.

I want to become the best version of myself and reach the pinnacle of my career, despite the obstacles I face, including the ones that are racial. However, that does not mean that racism does not exist, or it is an issue that should not be treated as urgent and critical. Because I had a White father and grew up around White-presenting people, I adopted White culture.

In the 1990s, acceptance was never an issue because my father did all he could to protect me and show that he cares about me. However, it was a different ball game when I got out there. There were uncomfortable stares and tongues wagging because of my ethnicity but who would believe my sad story? I know what my father would tell me if I reported the incidents to him. He would tell me to ignore the idiots and focus on my life and my goals. However, it was never that simple. I felt that it was not meant to be like that. I ought to be respected and treated as a White kid because of my father but it was not happening.

I never enjoyed the privileges I saw White-presenting people enjoy. It is not as though I wanted to be treated differently from others. I simply wanted to be treated the same way my White friends and family were treated. Why should I be expected to speak less or keep my opinions hidden because of the color of my skin? Why should I be treated as though my opinions do not matter, especially when I think differently? The pain of being treated like a second-class citizen was real, especially in my teenage years.

There are days that I look back and wonder how I was able to survive that period. All I wanted was for me to get the same respect that my White friends and family got. Why should I have to unnecessarily assert myself before people hear what I have to say or pay attention to me? I have to work hard and earn success before I can be respected and recognized but a White person doesn't have to try so hard. It was meant to be different since I had a White father but even that was not enough.

My Being Black

In the eyes of Western culture, I'm not seen as fully Black, more like a distracting racial curiosity by all races, which interferes with me being heard and understood. My Visual Minority family is very small. Compared to my White family, they aren't nearly as affluent, educated, or well-spoken, but I noticed when there is a crisis, they are far more engaging and willing to help than my White family, through their actions and not just their words. I tend to identify as Black to my Visual Minority friends and some of my White friends that share the same Visual Minority friends I do.

I was far more comfortable around my Visual Minority friends and Visual Minority family than my White family and friends. Unlike when I am with my White friends and family, I never have to try to assert myself when having conversations with them. Any lack of respect or regard had nothing to do with my skin color. I could be judged based on the validity and how logical my argument is rather than being misunderstood and expected to say something that doesn't make sense because I appear more Black than White. Initially, being around them was like my haven. Staying around them was that place I could be without being worried about the curious optics of my skin color.

It was comfortable initially, but I started getting concerned at some point. It felt like I was settling for less. My instinct told me that I should just stay more around the people that accept me easily, and shouldn't bother about the people that I feel I need to do more for before I can earn their respect. Still, I kept wondering why the world should be like that. Why should we just accept that some people's opinions about us will never change? If we were taught certain things in school that changed our perception, then we can change the way we think about racism.

If the world could move from thinking that the earth was flat to realizing that it is spherical, then there can be a shift in the way people see racism. I realized that many of my Visual Minority friends and family have come to accept that there will always be White-presenting people that would not respect them and treat them as equals. This is one of the reasons they are more comfortable being around people of their race. Just like me, it was their solace and haven.

However, I began to notice a pattern that was dangerous and that needed to stop. I started noticing that some of my Visual Minority friends agreed that they would never gain the acceptance and approval of White-presenting people, and this made them hostile toward them. Some assume that all White-presenting people are the same. They felt that even when a White-presenting person is not publicly using racial slang, he or she harbors resentment against Visual Minority people.

Of course, due to my experience and exposure, I knew that was not the truth. I have met some amazing White-presenting people because I have them as my friends and family. So, I realized that in the same way that White-presenting people don't have Visual Minority people in their close circles of friends is affecting their perception of Visual Minority people, the same can be said about Visual Minority people who do not have White-presenting people in their circles. Some of them have wrong ideas about White-presenting people because of some of the things they have been told by the people around them about White-presenting people.

So, I realized that it is not only racially active White-presenting people that should engage in conversations that will help to educate people from their race, but it is also the responsibility of racially active Visual Minorities to educate their people. Two wrongs wouldn't make a right. The fact that Visual Minority people are the minority doesn't mean that they should play victims by having wrong perceptions of White-presenting people. There are indeed White-presenting people that are racists, but many are not. Therefore, the battle against racism has to be fought from both ends.

It would not help matters if Visual Minority people are stereotypical in their perception of White-presenting people. My experience of the two worlds has made me realize that there is work to do on both sides. There is no doubt that Visual Minority people and other minority races are the victims of racism. They are the ones that know what it means to go through the street with the fear of being brutalized by the police because they appear threatening. They are also the ones that know the pain of being made to feel like second-class citizens in their own country.

My Being Jewish

I used to ponder... If God loves all races of people he created equally, why don't all races love each other equally as God does? I tried to identify as Jewish (knowing it is a religion, not a nationality but treated as a culture) as a kid. My being Jewish is synonymous with uncomfortable surprise or inappropriate fascination by White Jews. So, I've learned to hide it to avoid being questioned by White-presenting people about my religion. My father thought my being Jewish would bring me some prestige to help me as a mixed ethnicity child of the early 1980s, but he was wrong.

My bar mitzvah was uncomfortable. One guest and I weren't White-presenting but everyone else was. I felt uncomfortable inviting people I went to school with because I was the only Jew in the school, and I knew I would probably be the only Jew of color the people at my bar mitzvah would ever see, and I couldn't wait for it to be forgotten because I knew talking about it to my White-presenting Jewish father, and White-looking older brothers wouldn't get me the serious attention I craved. No one in my synagogue was a Visual Minority. Why?

Sadly, I couldn't talk about it because it made White-presenting people in my family feel uncomfortable.

Why doesn't Judaism refer to Visual Minority Jews, and therefore Black slavery? It only references White Jews' slavery. As a kid, I also noticed that when I went to a Jewish camp of hundreds that no one else was a Visual Minority. I was the only one. My last day in the synagogue was racially upsetting to me but was ignored when I tried to talk about it with my White father and White-presenting brother. A female Rabbi racially profiled me while I was waiting for my White family to leave the bathroom. Religion was meant to be the link between men of all races, but segregation still found a way to get into these circles.

My encounter with the female Rabbi was particularly emotionally disturbing because I had been taught to respect such people by my religion. They were supposed to be the beacon of hope in a broken world. Such people were meant to be epitomes of the concept of the equality of all men before God but that was not the case in this particular scenario. It was a moment that almost eroded my faith in God. The situation contradicted the Sunday School omnibenevolent teachings I had received for years, which didn't prepare me for a Rabbi to profile me and didn't prepare me for the modern-day sting of racism and its effects on inequality.

Chapter Two:
My Stories Of Invisibility Of Racism
(Racial Injustices)

Fortunately or unfortunately, I have had experiences of racial injustices at several points in my life. In some cases, I couldn't process what I was experiencing at that moment, but it made more sense as I grew older. In this chapter, I will go into detail regarding some of these experiences to help you have a better picture of the, sometimes invisible, nature of racial inequity.

A Brutal Introduction

My first subtle encounter with racist inequality came at the early age of six years old in the early 1980s. It was confusing and physically painful, as well as terrifying. In grade one, I knew a Caucasian bully named Roger. He had blonde hair and blue eyes, and he was bigger than I was. Roger and I lived in the same apartment building across the street from the same elementary school that we both attended, except that he was a couple of grades ahead of me. I'm not sure how our rivalry started, but we teased each other often. I said he was huge, and he said I was dumb. He always said that one day he would catch me and beat me up if he ever caught me (and at the time, I thought he was kidding, but unknown to me, he was dead serious).

Our rivalry continued for weeks, and one day Roger set a trap for me. I ran away from him that day and entered one of the very long hallways of our apartment building. I thought I had lost Roger by using the stairwell instead of the elevator, but when I exited the stairwell, there he was, blocking my path towards my apartment where I lived with my mother and grandmother. The look in his eyes was terrifying, like a starving predator looking at prey. I felt like I was in real trouble. I could hear my breath as I started to pant in fear, and the stress of the situation made my body feel heavy, and my legs felt like jelly. I knew my only option was to run the other way. However, Roger had coordinated his trap with a friend of his that cut me off in the other direction.

Now I was cornered with nowhere to go. I couldn't go up, I couldn't go down, I couldn't go left, I couldn't go right, so I made as much noise as possible, hoping someone would come out of their unit and scare these boys off, but nobody came. Things happened very quickly. They both closed in on my location. One of them shoved me, and I fell while the other kicked me in the face repeatedly. I felt my right eye had started to shut. I remember getting battered pretty much all over by both of them, but I had never lost sight in one of my eyes before and I was scared I was blind in one eye as I then felt my face swell up. The two boys ran away, and I was left bruised, bleeding, humiliated, and I had noticed they had kicked one of my teeth loose. My mouth and lips felt a bit tingly, and I felt my confidence was in free fall. I had never had a violent encounter like this before.

I knocked on the door of my home, and when my mother answered, she couldn't believe her eyes. She saw her son battered and beaten. She saw blood dripping from my mouth and blood staining my T-shirt, and part of my face was swollen. She pulled me inside and asked what happened, quite sternly. I said, Roger from school and one of his friends had beaten me up and I'm scared that they will do it again. My mother asked me where Roger lives. I said I don't know but I know he lives on the top floor above us in our building somewhere. She said, 'we're going to find this boy right now. Come on son, let's go!' I said to her, 'Shouldn't I clean myself up first?' And my mother said to me, with a mixture of pain and rage in her eyes that I had never seen before, 'No, I want them all to see the blood and the pain.'

With my mother being the strong person and formidable presence that she is, I didn't hesitate to follow her instructions, but it didn't help the fact that I felt humiliated every step of the way, showing my lumped-up face, door to door, but I trusted my mother and her judgment. So, off we went on our door-to-door campaign to find Roger and his family to have a discussion. We knocked on a lot of doors, and with each person opening their apartment door, I felt the look of them peering down on me in morbid curiosity, surprisingly lukewarm concern, and observing how my mother said, 'Do you know who Roger is? Roger has assaulted my child.' To this day, I don't know if these neighbors of mine were just in shock or afraid of my mother because no one admitted to knowing who Roger was.

Finally, and systematically, we found the correct apartment. I remember having to go to the bathroom very badly, feeling like we had been at this for hours. And when the door opened, there he was, Roger himself. Roger took a look at me and then took a look at my enraged mother, and at that moment, I saw that my schoolyard bully, whom I thought was my predator, had now become my mother's prey. I could see fear in his eyes, and I loved the feeling. I felt empowered and hoped I could take advantage of that moment to let him taste the bitter medicine he gave me earlier. It became obvious to me that we all feel fear at one point or another. In this case, it's only a matter of meeting someone more powerful than we are, that could trigger it. Roger and his friend had struck fear in my heart earlier. But there Roger was, looking sheepish and powerless, caught in the laser-like gaze of my mother.

I wished I could savor the moment a while longer. However, his parents soon showed up to ruin this beautiful moment for me. I thought it was going to be the beginning of the end for him, but I was wrong. To my surprise, my mother had been planning a lesson for me to learn while we were searching for Roger and his family and this was the moment she would reveal the purpose of her lesson to me because as soon as the door opened, she noticed that Roger and I had recognized each other. She knew this boy was the cause of my injuries, and she yelled at me to run over to Roger and 'hit him back now!' My mother said, 'Paul, you've got to hit him back, otherwise he will always pick on you. You have to let him know you're strong. Go get him, Paul, get him!'

I was surprised, and I froze because my cultural values were suddenly in conflict. As much as I wanted Roger to experience the same pain I had felt earlier, thanks to the malicious activity of him and his friend, I didn't want to be the one to inflict the pain on him. I had thought that my mother was going to deal with him or instigate his parents against him. I was just not ready to hit him back. My White family values taught me diplomacy and negotiation - or so I thought. I couldn't articulate this at the time, but my Visual Minority family values (at the time) were now teaching me that sometimes you have to fight because some people cannot be negotiated with and will never take you seriously.

Well, the bottom line is that, at that moment, I failed my mother's test and stayed frozen as Roger left the door open and ran away to see his parents in fear of my mother's reprisal. Roger's elderly parents came to the door and asked what happened. And that's where my mother piped up and said, 'Look at my child. Roger has beat up my child with his friend. Your son is an angry boy and planned a trap with his friend to corner my child and kick him in the face until his eye swelled shut and his tooth was nearly knocked out.' After hearing my mother speak, like a lawyer defending her client in court, I thought for sure I was going to get justice due to her brilliant opening statement in my defense.

26

I thought Roger was going to be punished, and the situation was going to be over, but I was wrong. I remember looking at Roger's parents expecting them to take action against their son, but instead, they looked at my mother like she was crazy, and they told her to calm down, and that their son would never do anything like that. They turned to Roger, who was hiding behind them, and said, 'did you do this?' Roger stayed quiet and transformed himself from this terrifying, violent child figure to a little innocent soul that seemed to have lost his way.

I was enraged because I knew no one seemed to be taking my mother or me seriously and I wondered why. After that, I remember Roger's parents and my mother arguing and watching my mother become more and more enraged. Finally, the door was shut, and my mother grabbed me by the arm, and we walked away back to our apartment where she cleaned me up and sat down with me as I iced my eye, waiting for the swelling to come down so I could see normally again, quietly hoping I wouldn't lose the tooth that Roger's boot loosened. I wasn't sure what had just happened exactly, but I knew my mother was very upset and I was still terrified that I was going to be hurt again, only next time even worse.

My mother and I just sat there in front of the television quietly. I was afraid to further upset her by talking about what happened, and she was no doubt calculating how to handle the situation. We knew this wasn't over. A couple of days passed, and we knocked on Roger's door again to have a conversation with Roger and his parents, only this time, my White-presenting father accompanied us. When the door opened, Roger's father opened the door and called his wife over. I remember they both looked at me and my mother plainly, but when Roger's parents saw my father, their eyes widened, and I listened carefully as Roger's parents were very ingratiating to my father as he calmly yet angrily said that the assault on me must be taken very seriously.

I noticed whenever my father spoke, Roger's parents didn't interrupt, they never condescended, and they never challenged my White father like they did my Visual Minority mother. After listening to my father, they even yelled at Roger and said, "You're grounded!" But even after seeing my mother for the second time, they never seemed to take my mother seriously, and they never seemed to take me seriously. They never asked me how I was feeling, and they never apologized to my mother for closing the door on her at our last encounter. However, they did apologize to my father, and Roger was grounded but only after my White-presenting father had done the talking for us (a Visual Minority family).

For years after that, I was confused, and I wasn't sure who I could talk to (and be understood) about the fact that I felt I had just witnessed a racial injustice. I never forgot feeling that the only reason why Roger left me alone was that my White-presenting father used his White privilege to defend my Visual Minority mother and me from being ignored. By the way, we never found Roger's friend who helped him beat me up.

When I First Suspected The Existence Of White Privilege

When I was 8, in the produce section of the grocery store, I remember my father would eat a grape or a strawberry here and there from what seemed to me like a mountain of food at the time. Initially, I never thought much about it, but after a while, I said to him, "Dad, you can't do that, isn't that stealing?" He laughed a bit and quickly replied, "It's okay Paul. The grocery store expects some of the products they sell won't sell, they call it shrinkage." His explanation sounded logical and calming to me. I had never seen or heard of anyone else taking something so confidently before paying for it, and not seeming to mind before. So, I took that lesson as permission to copy my father.

So, there we were, father and son, walking through the grocery store and taking food we had not paid for yet. My father didn't seem to have a problem with it, but I couldn't bring myself to feel as comfortable as he seemed to be and I wasn't sure why. After many weekend trips to the grocery store with him, at times, I noticed I felt like I was being watched whenever I took a sample of food (the same thing my father always did, only for me, there was a social consequence that he didn't have to endure). Without consciously being aware, fate seemed to test this situation for me.

One day, my father and I were in the grocery store and he was in one aisle sampling a strawberry and I was in another aisle sampling a grape, and an elderly White lady said to me, "Excuse me young man but what you're doing is wrong." I looked up at her and said, "My father does it all the time" (as I pointed with my eyes and nod of my chin in the direction of his location). She looked at me, she looked at my father, and seemed surprised and just kept on walking and ignoring him as she passed him by. My father paid no attention to her and kept on sampling. I was aggravated and confused.

I asked myself if she had a problem with me taking food, why didn't she have the same problem with my father, who is right beside us, taking food in another aisle? I felt singled out. After that, I became more sensitive to the feeling of being watched in the grocery store by some of the store staff and some of the other customers for years as I keenly observed my father act as though he did not share any of these feelings.

I Witnessed My First Display Of Symbolic Racism

My first day of high school started very excitingly. Not only was I stepping into a new chapter of life, but I was also lucky enough to attend a brand-new high school. At the time, the school was known as 'the school of the future' with the latest and greatest technology and athletic facilities. Up until that time, my Visual Minority friends and I used to play a lot of basketball. We spent many summers competing against each other and challenging other players to play us. I remember playing all day, even into the night. I played so much that when I got home at night after playing all day, it wasn't until I flipped on the lights of the bathroom to wash my hands that I realized how much effort I had put in that day by seeing how black my hands were from handling the basketball.

Anyway, my Visual Minority friends and I were excited to hear about an outdoor basketball court specially built for high school students at our new school, and we decided to check out the court and play as we usually do. On the way to the court, we saw for the first time just how incredible our new school outdoor facilities were. We had never seen a football field or a rubber running track and now a new basketball court to behold. The sight was so exciting, especially for me. However, when we got there, to my surprise, I noticed that this brand-new basketball court already had its first blemish. In the center of the court floor, someone or some people had spray-painted a large white-colored circle with a certain cross in the middle that I had never seen before.

At the time, I didn't know what it was, but I remember feeling disappointed that this brand-new court had already seen graffiti, but I ignored it as we played on. Still, this new shape was like a bug in my brain. The next day, during my lunch, I heard a lot of people saying that the graffiti symbol on the basketball court was a White supremacist symbol, and right away, I felt a lump in my throat and quite a bit of rising fear in my gut.

I heard a few terrible stories about the KKK from my father, and I wasn't sure if this symbol was foretelling I might encounter another violent bully, only this time, a racist one. I never told anybody I was nervous about this symbol being the beginning of a possible lynching because my instincts told me no one would take me seriously. I remember saying to my Visual Minority friends, "I can't believe somebody would do this, especially that they would stereotypically believe that placing this symbol on a basketball court would send a message to as many Visual Minority people as possible that they are not welcome here in a free and public place (or so I thought), which includes me. And the worst part was that it worked!

I stopped playing basketball altogether as a result, and I avoided that basketball court for a long time. Even after a year from then, the thought of seeing that symbol again made me feel sick. The school tried to cover it up by spray-painting over the graffiti with a slightly different shade of green to blend in with the rest of the green background of the court, but they got the shade wrong, and it was very easy to see what was still there. To this day, I don't know why they didn't just clean it and make an announcement that this behavior was racist and unacceptable. It was as though people just quietly forgot about it and turned their backs.

However, that was harder for me to do since this basketball court was on my path home. It was then that I decided to switch my interest from basketball to volleyball to avoid feeling like I was hated and unwelcome by whoever sent this message. I was secretly angry at my principal for not addressing this crime of hatred. In my mind, the racists won that round and never had any reason to worry about any consequences. They were free to send another message if they chose to.

I Tested The Existence Of White Privilege In School

In 10th grade, I became a little bolder and angrier as I began to sense the invisibility of inequality subtly affecting me. I didn't know how to articulate it peacefully, but I knew that something was unfair, and something was wrong in my world, and I felt I had something to prove to be understood and that people in my White-presenting family and my White-presenting friends didn't have to endure this invisible force, and that frustrated me. I felt like how a dog can feel pain but can't communicate it to anyone. I started spending more time making White-presenting friends. I wasn't planning it consciously, but I felt that if I had more White-presenting friends, their privilege and entitlement may rub off on me, but I was wrong. Maybe it would have been easier if I weren't the only Jew in school, but I'll never know for sure.

Later in the school year, I became close friends with a White-presenting person. Much of his family was from Germany, and he had blond hair and blue eyes. We were like brothers. We looked out for one another and he was (and still is) a great friend. Still, when I tried to explain a hint of the existence of invisible inequality, he didn't believe me. We were in English class, and I said to him in some off-hand remark that I feel like, with certain teachers, I have to work twice as hard to get half the grades that he gets because of the way I look.

When my friend heard that, he practically erupted in a way that he thought was protecting me from exploring that belief. He said, "No way! That can't be true. If you work hard, you'll succeed." And I said to him, "But what if you're not given the chance to work hard? What if a decision is already made about you and it doesn't matter how hard you work? How can you succeed if you're not given the chance to work hard in the first place?" He was confused and had no answer, and I wasn't sure if I was more confused than he was - all I knew was something didn't feel right.

In this English class, we were in, I worked my heart out and felt I could never get ahead no matter what I did. I stayed after school, I worked with the teacher, I put in the hours, I followed instructions to the best of my ability and still, I could never get an A. With every assignment, I got a B minus or a C plus. This was a trend for me, to work hard and wonder why I'm not succeeding and look around and see others like my friend get a consistent A. By comparison, they didn't seem to work as hard as I did after school time. Finally, I got so frustrated I said to my friend, "Let's test my theory. I'll write your essay, and you write my essay, and we'll see who gets the better grade." My friend said, "Okay."

I felt supercharged with motivation to see what would happen. Questions started bubbling up in my mind. Can racism infect my teachers, and if so, how could that affect my grades, and therefore my future, and therefore my

34

academic ability to succeed? Such big questions eventually gave me a headache and caused a bit of anxiety, so I just focused on the work instead. I spent 40 hours working on my essay, and I wrote it out by hand because I didn't have a computer. When I was done, I typed it up at my friend's house since he had a computer, and I watched as he wrote his essay right in front of me. It took him two hours. We switched our names on the essays as we said we would, and we handed them in the next day to the same English teacher, a teacher who I was convinced didn't see me as smart as my friend (for some reason, I wasn't sure exactly why, but I thought it was because he looked more important because he was White).

A few days later, we received our marks back. My friend got an A- and I got a C+ or should I say, my 40-hour handwritten then typed essay got an A- and my friend's two-hour essay got a C+. In class, we sat beside each other. As I looked at both papers side by side, I felt a combination of rage and relief. Relief that my instincts were right, rage that I was being treated unfairly and had no way to solve it without creating new problems of teacher/student perception I couldn't anticipate. I watched very closely as my friend's eyes widened as he looked at the papers. To me, it looks like the construct of his beliefs and perceptions of what is normal were crumbling down. Even though we lacked the language to fully identify it, he and I had just realized, with evidence in hand, that White privilege exists and is alive and well.

He said to me, "This must've been a fluke. This doesn't make any sense." So, I said, "Then let's try again." He said, "Okay, but I think the result is going to be different this time. I'll try to work on my essay, and I bet the results will be about the same." I said, "You're on buddy, only this time, let's make it more interesting. This time, let's each make up a word and put it in our essays and see if the teacher notices it on both of our papers." He laughed and said okay.

Well, that's exactly what we did. We worked side-by-side from beginning to end and created what we thought were two pretty good essays. We each spent about 5 to 10 hours on our essays. My made-up word was 'plasticated.' It meant to intentionally make something natural be seen and felt as artificial. My friend's made-up word was 'evility.' I'm not sure what the contextual meaning was but it didn't matter because, in my mind, the trap for invisible inequality had again been set.

As before, we handed in our papers and awaited the results. When we got our papers back, we saw the same result as before. The paper with my friend's name on it got an A, and the paper with my name on it got a B (some minor improvement - I'm sure you caught that), only this time, the teacher red-circled the made-up word with my name on it, but not on the other paper. She missed my friend's made-up word altogether. Again, I was very upset. To me, there was now double the evidence that racism still exists and it's staring at me, only now (unlike my father's KKK stories), it had taken on a subtle and quiet form. Yet, I still felt I had no one to support me on this, much less understand my feelings or my position.

I held my resolve until after class when I said to my friend, "This is the way it is; White kids get better grades just because they are White. Sometimes, it doesn't matter how hard you work." - Just as I said that a White-presenting supply teacher two steps behind me aggressively included herself in our conversation and said, "That's just not true." My friend was quiet and looked very confused and I just rolled my eyes, but I was now secretly worried for my academic future. At the end of the school year, our English teacher asked my friend if she could keep a copy of his essay as an example of good writing to use in future classes. He said, "That's okay," and in my mind, I said to the English teacher, "You're welcome!" I was never angry at my teacher. I liked her, but again I knew something wasn't right. In her class, I felt like the cards had been stacked against me. Oh, and by the way, our English teacher was a Visual Minority.

Chapter Three:
More Stories Of Invisibility Of Racism

In the previous chapters, I discussed more of my experiences of invisible racial inequity in my younger years. In this section, I will cite more examples of such situations to give you a better picture of how it could be difficult for anyone who is not observant enough to notice racial inequity, where racism is politically incorrect and seen as socially unacceptable behavior.

When Thoughts Of Inequality Hit Close To My Home

Two years after my encounter with my English teacher, another incident involving my neighbor (a Visual Minority man) suffering from depression and schizophrenia, who was shot dead by officers in 1996, made me more scared than ever. A Coroner's jury returned a verdict of homicide and recommended that all officers should be required to take a course on crisis resolution, and I wonder if the outcome would still be non-lethal if my Visual Minority neighbor was White-presenting. And could that happen to me one day? I remember him clearly. He was a good-looking guy and extremely athletic, and physically strong. I remember he and his brother played basketball in their driveway and one day; they asked me to play with them.

My neighbor (the one who was shot) said to me and his brother, "You guys can face me." I laughed out loud and said, "Hey, I'm a bit rusty but I'm not terrible" (I knew his brother and he was also athletic). They both smiled at me and I soon realized why. There was nothing I or his brother could do. My neighbor was like an athletic artist - he found ways to sneak past us or push us back. I was so impressed. He never seemed to tire and just kept passively smiling as he embarrassed us over and over. It was like I was being taken back to school in realizing how my game needed a lot more work than I thought. After we were beaten badly, I shook his hand to show there were no hard feelings. He gave me a handshake that was so strong, that it felt like a freezer burn.

When I heard the news that he was shot multiple times and killed by police, I felt extremely sad for his family and secretly terrified that this struck so close to home. Our mothers (my neighbor's and mine) were close friends, and my mother told me something about this situation that didn't feel right. I asked her to explain what happened. To this day, I don't have all the details, but from what I can recall, my mother said he was mentally ill and was found on the street smashing windows with something in his hand. The police were called, drew their weapons, and asked him to drop whatever was in his hand (I assumed the police were trained to give suspects every chance to surrender before deciding to open fire), and then turn around. He turned around first without dropping whatever was in his hand, and the officers shot him.

Four years later, an article was written about the incident. The SIU (Special Investigations Unit) cleared the officers involved of all charges. A Coroner's jury returned a verdict of homicide and recommended that all officers be required to take a course in Crisis Resolution and that police test and research non-lethal weapons, including the taser. If officers saw a White-presenting man instead of a Visual Minority man, would the officers feel less compelled to fire? Would the officers have felt a White-presenting person would be less of a threat? Back then, I secretly thought, could the officers have been influenced by social norms to see Visual Minority people as more threatening than any other race? And if that's true, could this happen to me one day? I don't look White. It terrified me. Well, those thoughts (unbeknownst to me) were going to be tested.

Fear Of White Cops

About three years onward, I was driving home from my father's cottage like I had many times before, but this time it was later in the evening. I remember I took the back roads instead of the highway, and I noticed there was a police car on the side of the road as I drove by. Well, it didn't take long before I was pulled over. While waiting for the officer to speak to me, I immediately started self-diagnosing what the reason for being pulled over could have been. Was I speeding? Was there something wrong with my car? Or was there something wrong with me? I could think of no smoking-gun reason for being stopped. I shut the engine down. I was nervous, but that was all. I noticed two White officers were in the car parked behind me. One of the officers came out of the car and started walking towards me with his hand on his gun. And it looked like he was turned slightly to the side as he oddly walked towards my car.

My nervousness turned into fear. I rolled the window down and tried to stick my head out of the window to say something friendly. I think I tried to say something neutral like "is there a problem sir?" But before I could get all of the words out, the officer yelled, "Eyes forward! Put your hands on the wheel!" Well, at that moment, I noticed my fear blooming into terror. My left leg started to jitter, and I could feel myself sweating from the armpits. I did what I was told but the stress led me right back to thinking of my neighbor being shot to death by police. The thought that a similar nightmare is now unfolding right in front of me filled my mind, and that was overwhelming. Now, I don't want to sound overdramatic, but I thought this could escalate to my death, and I had no reason to think otherwise as I watched the officer carefully step his way to me through my side mirror with his hand still poised over his weapon. I felt my heart beating out of my chest. I felt trapped and helpless in an endless moment of silence.

When the officer got to me, he shined a flashlight into my eyes and asked me where I came from and where I was going. I told him the truth in a very uneasy tone of voice. He sounded so angry - his tone of voice just added to my anxiety. He asked for my license and insurance. I was scared to ask if it was okay to take my hands off the wheel to get it. I could feel him staring past my eyes to the back of my head, like a predator. Luckily, I had everything ready to go. All my papers were kept in a plastic folder in a compartment on the driver's door. I opened the folder in my lap. Just then, the officer abruptly said, "Give that to me - I'll take that." I handed him the open folder. In the spine of the folder was some dirt, dust, etc.

He pointed at the dirt in the spine of the folder and said, "What's this?" I said, "It looks like dirt sir." He sneered at me and then put his flashlight away and did the strangest thing. He licked his finger and used it to touch the dirt and taste it (I guess he thought he was about to bust me for drugs or something). He walked away with the binder back to his car. I could see him and his partner talking in my rearview mirror. I felt relief that I might not be killed. Instead, just wrongfully hauled off to jail without knowing my rights. I didn't know what to do or say. I had a headache, I felt tired and anxious, and I badly needed to go to the bathroom.

I waited in the car for what felt like a very long time. The police car then drove up to my window - our cars were almost touching. I was convinced this problem was about to multiply but thankfully, I was wrong. The other White officer in the passenger seat (the one that stayed in the car) handed my folder back to me and said, "Here you go, sir." I was too terrified to say anything back. The older White officer who investigated me looked like he was annoyed, as he kept his eyes forward and didn't look back at me. However, as I looked back at the other officer who handed me the folder, he quietly mouthed the word

"Sorry," and just as I took the folder back, they drove away. I felt like I was going to explode. I got out of the car and relieved myself on the side of the road. Then, I sat in the car waiting for my heart to stop pounding, and I also thought that waiting would put more needed distance between me and that experience.

The next day I told a Visual Minority friend what had happened while at work and on a lunch break. He listened carefully, then said, "That's terrible Paul, that officer was not on your side." Just then, we were interrupted by someone we work with. He was a very tall White-presenting man (who later became my friend). After inviting himself into our conversation, he forcefully said, "Ya know Paul, the cop was just doing his job, so don't make a big deal out of it." When I heard that, I became quite enraged. I thought, first, how a person can rudely invite himself into a conversation without witnessing the context of it. Second, I didn't give this person permission to enter the conversation and form an opinion that belittles me, especially when his skin color (as a White-presenting man) will never interfere with people taking him seriously enough to listen. Third, clearly, at this moment, this person prioritized opinion over compassion.

Later in the day, I said to him, have you been stopped by the police without reason in a way that caused you to fear for your life? He laughed and walked away. It took months for me to realize this persons' White privilege may have caused his compassionate blindness because it seemed he had no similar and painful reference to what

I experienced. It may have caused a bias in his perception of the invisibility of inequality.

By comparison to being pulled over by White officers, a couple of years later, a Visual Minority officer pulled me over for not completely stopping at a stop sign. As soon as I saw the police car coming, I remember saying out loud, "Oh sh*t!" I instantly knew what I had done. I was nervous about the punishment I would receive but I never felt my life was in danger. The Visual Minority officer told me why he pulled me over straight away, gave me a hefty ticket, and said, "Have a better day."

It took a bit of reflection but after that, I thought about the difference between both officers' situations. And this time, life had sent me a wonderfully scientifically controlled experiment. What I mean is, the variables were the same in both police cases: me, the car I was driving, the city I was driving in, and therefore the same police division (or staff)... except for one variable: the skin color of the officers. But I wasn't sure I could prove to myself that it mattered. All I knew was what I realized about myself. I realized this experience had taught me to fear White-presenting police officers, and generally question who the police may tend to serve and protect the most. It made me wonder if I ever called the police for protection, might certain officers be less motivated to serve and protect me based on the color of my skin?

In reflection, I couldn't ask the White officer a question without fearing reprisal from him and danger, when I'm certain my White-presenting father wouldn't be interrupted like I was if he were in my position (which helped me understand why he appeared to be more confident than I was) - he faced lower socially norming consequences than I did. I would come to hypothesize this kind of inequality as White entitlement.

I Realized I Wasn't As Keen On Spotting Ignorance As I Thought

In 2008, two of my Visual Minority friends and I wanted to sail small boats in Toronto, and we found a series of small sailing clubs in a remote downtown area. We interviewed some of the members, asked questions, and got a read on whether or not we would socially fit in amongst the existing members. I, for one, focused only on how great it would be to sail in the city. It all seemed to check out, the price, the people, all of it, except that I was deeply involved in earning a Jiu-Jitsu Black Belt at the time. So, I promised to return to the club after I had achieved my 1st Dan and could then totally focus on sailing (something I already had a lot of experience with, but I hid that experience to make new friends easier, without coming across as an expert).

I kept my promise to myself. I earned my Black Belt, and between then and when I joined the sailing club in 2011, I met my partner and insisted we join together. A few summers passed and I thought I had found a haven of nice people. And most of them were and still are. My point is, I detected zero feelings of racism from anyone, despite the club being almost completely composed of White-presenting people (which was expected since, to me, sailing is historically and traditionally perceived as a predominantly White persons' activity). It was 2017 and I had presumably thought (up to then) that no one of the 200 members had a reason to dislike me. Perhaps that was a bit of conceit. Another Visual Minority friend and I (the only two brown club members at the time that I can recall) decided to throw a party for the entire club and its guests. All would be welcome.

The plan was for all of us to be outdoors and to serve lamb, chicken, vegetables, salads, and soup using only fire to do the cooking as a community (where anyone could help if they wanted to). Together, we engineered, built, and tested a makeshift stone oven and timed how long it would take to achieve and maintain the heat we needed to cook for an estimated minimum group of 60 people for 3 hours. I would bring my live wedding band to play as entertainment. I would sing and give salsa dance lessons and help with the cooking and my friend would source the meat and also cook. We aimed to break even by charging a reasonable amount per ticket at cost. We put a team of wonderful volunteers together to create a special event to be proud of.

Word spread about our project, and unbeknownst to me, a group of older-aged members was writing letters to the board each week saying my friend and I should be ashamed for using this party to steal money from the club by profiting from ticket sales.

I had never worked harder as a volunteer for a non-profit event before in my life. The party was partially on my mind for the better part of a year. In my mind, the party was a success. With limited resources, no existing budget or experience, and on our first try, my friend and I did together what a seasoned team of party planners would have trouble executing. While at the party, I couldn't find an unhappy face even if I tried. Finally, I realized how deeply offended some of the older members were with us when the commodore of the club told me that some people think we should be publicly shamed for our efforts.

At the clubs' annual general meeting, I listened to hours of intense debate back and forth between the older-aged and younger-aged members. The older-aged members accused us of profiteering and didn't attend our party. By contrast, the younger-aged members who did attend our party (including the volunteers who sold the tickets) said our party was above board. The argument went round and round. One person would say we are the villains, another would say the opposite. I felt sick to my stomach and betrayed by the very same club I spent my valuable time working hard to feed and entertain. Soon, my White-presenting partner began to cry, and I felt very hurt seeing her tears fall. So why am I telling you this? Well, a moment came that made me realize that my intuition about people's nature was a bit blind.

To my surprise and appreciation, a very articulate friend of mine stood behind the lectern and addressed the club. He said, "Why are we condemning these two members for giving us this party when the board has said their party was legitimate?" He then went on to say that years ago, he remembered when another fire-cooked food party was provided to the club by another club member resulting in zero emotional meetings like this. He then strongly intimated that the only difference between the person who threw the party years ago and the people who threw the same party now was the color of their skin.

I quickly scanned the room and for a long-lasting moment, the room went dark with silent thought and wide-eyed discomfort. To me, my friend may have temporarily exposed the dirty laundry of the clubs' collective psyche. I had just realized that I might have been blind to spotting the invisibility of racial ignorance in people that I thought liked me. Still, I couldn't help but feel I was being tolerated by some of the older-aged members up until now, and by extension of that feeling, I should know my place. At that moment, I felt the dark shadow of racism in the room, and I felt that it was squarely landing on the shoulders of my friend and me. It was humiliating for me, but my party planning partner seemed to be very cool and neutral. Later, I was told by a sailing club friend that we have to plan another party again (presumably to show we will not be oppressed). I tried to gather volunteers but after this experience, no one was willing to volunteer because they didn't want to be associated with our party again for fear of another reprisal.

My White Partner's Awakening To Invisible Inequality

In 2019, my partner and I had already taken many wonderful trips together. I had become much more comfortable with airport protocols, and my partner had taken an active attempt in struggling to understand 'invisible inequality.' After the sailing club party experience, I decided to step up my game and create a vacation for my closest sailing club friends and me, instead of just a party. I wanted to share my love of surfing and the country of Costa Rica with my people. Again, it took the better part of a year planning for this event, but I also loved including my friends to help with the planning as a community here and there, but the vision and what we do, where and how much it would cost was essentially up to me. My partner was engaged with flight research, accommodations, and accounting (thank goodness).

I gravitated towards activities, schedules, cost, and safety. Again, another memorable and action-packed event was born and tested to reuse and expand on. I was in my element and my friends could see the appeal in a country my partner and I are planning to move to one day. As all things came to a close, there we were in the Liberia airport of Costa Rica, standing in a long line as a group to check our bags and return home to Toronto. We were a group of two Visual Majorities, three identifiable Asians (two oriental and one south-eastern) and then there was me. Standing next to them, I probably looked like a local Costa Rican surfer or something, or someone no one has ever seen before. Just then, I could feel my instincts telling me I was being stared at, only this time, my White friend noticed something strange as well.

As I recall, a woman who worked at the airport came over to me and started asking questions. Where are you going, who are you traveling with, etc.? The questions sounded above board, but they were only directed at me - the rest of my group was ignored. I kept smiling but my awareness engine started turning like a propeller of an airplane. Still, I played it cool to not upset myself or my group. As I look back at this moment, even though I suspected a racial profiling encounter forming, my guard was almost completely down because I thought I visually blended in with the Costa Ricans.

But later, as we all passed through the X-ray scanners, I was the last to pass through security when two officers quickly approached and stopped me. My mind screamed, "Here we go again, I've had enough of this sh*t!" Normally, I'd behave in a soft and peaceful and ingratiating way as a sign of deference but this time, I was annoyed with the situation. The two officers started asking me more questions. Where, what, who, why, etc. I became an answering robot, looking at them with a neutral half-dead gaze, giving monotone one-word answers as often as I could. My partner then realized I was not at her side. I watched as she instantly surmised that I was being profiled, and for the first time in her life, she was watching it happen - and not only that, it was happening to me.

It was like time slowed down as I saw in her face, the realizations of all of my inequality stories were provable at this moment, and now things had gotten real for her via me. She now had the evidence and experience she needed to feel a bit of sympathetic fear.

She ran over and stood beside me and faced the officers, and I watched as they looked at her, looked at me and then let me go. Just as I was on my way again, one of the officers asked me, "Did you enjoy yourself in Costa Rica?" I said I thought I had but now I'm not sure. In my mind, my partner had been awakened to invisible inequality. Now she had somewhat of a personal reference to draw on. She told our friends what had happened right away. In response, I said I realized I felt I was under attack and I needed to relax.

I thanked my partner for using her White privilege to help give me access to pass through the profiling. Understandably, she wasn't sure how to respond. My last thought as we boarded the plane was about my partner. I said in my mind to her: now that you've felt a bit of emotional pain in this area, I know you won't forget it, and fortunately, it will help you, not just to agree, but to understand. I'm grateful for that.

Peacefully Speaking Out For The First Time

In 2021, my dog was playing in the park with another dog owned by a White-presenting owner. I was separated from the other dog owner by about 30 feet. A White officer drove his car off-road into the park and onto the grass towards me within about 6 feet - and not towards the White-presenting owner to tell me to leash my dog, but only 'suggested' the other owner do the same. I noticed this event contained the same situation, the same location, but yielded two different outcomes (one for me and the other for the other dog owner). The outcome for me was intimidation by the police, but the White-presenting dog owner didn't appear intimidated by the officer at all. The officer smiled at her and said, "Have a good day," and I was left feeling like I needed to get home immediately as I might be fined by this officer if I stayed.

Not long after that experience, one weekend, my home city of Toronto in April 2021 issued temporary enhanced police powers to indefinitely profile citizens during the Covid19 pandemic lockdown, which made me feel as though my rights and freedoms as a citizen of Canada were taken away. These enhanced powers gave the individual officer the permission and the right to racially profile citizens if and whenever they chose, with lawful justification and without consequence. The provincial government was attempting to curfew citizens in an attempt to impossibly control the spread of COVID-19 instead of prioritizing herd immunity through vaccination. But what I found ironic was that all of the politicians who were convinced this was the solution were White-presenting. And it made me wonder how many times in their lives had they felt the sting of wrongful and unnecessary racial profiling firsthand?

I took to Facebook and my post was read aloud on the legislative channel in Toronto for the caucus to hear by my local MPP politician Z. Thank you, Chris! I can't take credit for this, but by the end of that weekend, the premier recanted his opinions and legislation and apologized to the province of Ontario, Canada. This was what I said:

"As an Unidentifiable Visual Minority man, this new Toronto police enhanced powers make me nervous that the probability for me encountering racial profiling has now significantly risen. Three months ago, an officer drove off-road and into the park where I was standing to remind me to keep my dog on a leash. - I gotta walk my dog now, wish me luck...

As circumstances intensified, the next day, I wrote:

"Toronto Police Officers are now officially operating 'above the law' indefinitely and completely. What mechanisms exist to protect Visual Minority people from angry, ignorant, and emotional racial profiling? Or worse? Officers may now racially profile by choice, and fine 750 dollars if they choose without any foreseeable repercussions. But the officer's just doing his or her job, right? Lol. My White father would say: 'It's your word against theirs Paul.' It's hard to understand this if you present as White, but I now have to prepare what to do, say, behave, posture, observe, avoid, to keep a low profile whenever I leave my home indefinitely because I feel like my rights and freedoms may be tested."

In closing to this final story, I was relieved to see in the media how quickly many police regions openly rejected using their enhanced powers before they were removed. But this experience shouted to me that there's much more work yet to be done in educating our current White political leaders to see through the eyes of Visual

Minority people and to think consequentially before taking action. Conversely and positively, I also saw this experience as a call to action for all Visual Minority people, to consider making political leadership their career and duty, to help provide the government with more of a culturally diverse, wise perspective, to make inspiring decisions our citizens can be proud of.

As I said, it's hard to understand this if you present as White, but at the time, I had to prepare what to do, say, how to behave, posture, observe, avoid, to keep a low profile whenever I left my home because I felt like my rights and freedoms may be tested. It was hard enough to feel free even when you have not committed an offense as a half-white person who presents as an unidentifiable minority, especially when around White-presenting cops. That brief time felt like a decoy to strip Visual Minority people of their already socially limited rights and freedom.

I'm hopeful this will not happen again. But I would not be surprised if this led to more harassment of Visual Minority people in Canada. Of course, it is necessary to make laws that would protect people from spreading the infection. The basis for the law is commendable. However, the execution is not right. It makes the motive of creating the law questionable when it is Visual Minority people that are victims of profiling. It feels like someone who had always been looking for an opportunity to mistreat some people, finally got the opportunity to do what has always been on their mind. Of course, I don't expect this illustration to make perfect sense to you as a White-presenting person because you may have no idea what it feels like, first-hand, to be targeted because of your skin color.

Rabbi Racial Profiling

As a young man, my last day in the synagogue was upsetting to me. Since then, I have never returned. From when I was 5 to the age of 13, I went to Sunday school. I learned all about the Jewish holidays, customs, and culture. I spent my final 3 years teaching myself how to read and sing my Hebrew bar mitzvah portion during weekdays, living with my non-Jewish Visual Minority mother, and I practiced even more on the weekends for my White Jewish father – it was a significant grind because - looking back, I spent more time on that than I did working on my non-Jewish academics. It felt like there wasn't enough time to please both masters and teaching yourself how to sing and read a foreign language on weeknights alone at age 10 wasn't easy, and at the end of that period, I had my bar mitzvah.

I was relieved to finally get it out of the way. For years after that, my White-presenting father and one of my white-presenting brothers went to synagogue together traditionally, every year, for the New Year holidays. I secretly dreaded it. It was long, boring, uncomfortable, and I wasn't allowed to interact with anyone. So, I had no friends in the congregation since my Sunday school friends were a no-show.

But one day, the cycle was broken. In my mind, there came a moment that changed me. It left me feeling disappointed in my religion and I never returned to synagogue again. Here's the story. I must have been in my late teens or early twenties. For me, after a standard two-hour visit to the synagogue where praying, standing up, and sitting down were the highlights, while reading passages I couldn't find wisdom in, joined with the silent formality of not being able to speak to my family or others, was the norm, I was happy to leave that day.

My father and brother went into the bathroom and I waited for them outside the bathroom. So, there I was, still bored, and trying to pass the time by looking at black and white pictures of wise-looking Rabbis of the past and their colleagues (everyone was white of course) when I heard someone say, 'Excuse me?'

I thought I was blocking someone from passing me, so I spun around to apologize but there was no such interference. There she was, one of the Rabbis with a strange look on her face. Her expression reminded me of a Human Resources person trying to force a smile but whose intent was to deliver unsavory news.

I said something neutral like, "Is there something wrong?" She said, "Can I help you?" I said, "No thanks" – smiled back (I probably appeared as artificial as she did) and started to turn away, back to looking at the pictures of white-only strangers on the wall, when she persisted.

She then said, "Are you lost?" I turned back to her and noticed her expression was now slightly less smiley. I replied, "No I'm not lost, I'm waiting for my father and brother – thanks." I was a little aggravated, but I shook it off instantly. Just as I began to once again pretend to find interest in the photos - the Rabbi said to me in a partially condescending yet motherly tone: "Are you Jewish?"

Inside me, something snapped. An alarm went off – this felt personal. At that moment, elemental thoughts and base questions quickly bubbled up to the surface. Questions like, don't you see I'm wearing a dark-coloured suit and dress shoes like everyone else? Don't you see I'm wearing a Yarmulke on my head like everyone else in this place? At that moment, I felt like an exposed nerve. I felt like she was trying to single me out – and she succeeded in doing so. I felt myself becoming a mixture of angry and sad – because in my mind, I had spent years earning the right to call myself Jewish and I thought up until then that I was just as recognizably Jewish as everyone else – everything felt wrong at that moment.

I was tongue-tied. Here was this person I was taught to revere and respect without ever having to get to know and didn't have to earn my respect. She was a figurehead that I never expected would make me feel like I didn't belong. This awkward moment lasted a long time when I said to her – "Yes, I'm Jewish – that's why I'm here. Is there a problem?"

She smiled a smile that said, "How cute is this kid?" As I watched her seem to hold back a little bit of a laugh, my White father and white-presenting brother came out from behind the bathroom door that the Rabbi and I were standing beside.

I looked at them with relief (as though they had come to save me from this humiliating situation I can't explain) as they privately laughed about something they were talking about. My father said to me, "Come on Paul, let's go." Other than that, they paid me no notice. But I turned to face the Rabbi (now feeling as though my police backup had arrived) – there it was, my story for my presence checked out okay, and now that my evidence standing there was true, I was curious to see how the Rabbi would react.

The Rabbi took one look at my White-presenting father, and white-presenting brother, and simply turned around silently and walked in the opposite direction. She didn't even flash me a look – it was as if her emotions drained out of her as she walked away. I wanted to say something in my defense, but I felt caught off guard. Things happened so fast, and I never saw this coming. I was stressed.

In my mind, I thought, if this is how my religion will treat me when my White-presenting family isn't around, then it's time to give my religion back to where it came from. As we walked towards the parking lot – I felt myself becoming enraged. I didn't know what to do – I thought – is this how Rabbis act? Or is this how THIS Rabbi acts? Is religious racism a thing? If so, was it pointed at me? I don't have the free access to being at synagogue as I thought I did. Was having a white father and white-presenting brother beside me the only shield I had to be singled out? The internal over-analysis continued until my brother said – "Paul, are you okay?"

I said, "No I'm not okay. I think that Rabbi was racist toward me." Both of their faces dropped to the floor. My father said, "What happened?" I explained it all the best way I could, fumbling over every articulation (or so it felt). My brother was silent and seemed to defer to our father. My father said, "Ya know what Paul, the Rabbi didn't mean anything by it – no one's racist here" (in a calming yet authoritative tone of voice). I said, "No, she thought I was trespassing. She made me feel like I didn't belong when no one was looking. And then, when you two showed up, she walked away without an apology! Is that how a Rabbi should act? Why didn't she ask the two of you if you were Jewish?! This is wrong!"

I felt my emotions rise and rumble. My White-presenting father said again, "Paul, no one is out to get you, okay?" (He said with a distinct touch of anger in his voice). My brother stayed silent, and then I went silent as I listened to our father huff and puff for a short while.

To my father, I was being disrespectful, but to me, I was being honest, and, sadly, my father may have been focused on my tone and not my words. To this day, I wonder what my White-presenting brother was thinking and why he stayed silent – to this day he does not remember this story. I love my family, but I admit I was disappointed in them that day. I was taught to respect my religion and never question its wisdom, but after that day, and in my mind, I felt I had evidence and reason to question it anytime I wanted.

Ultimately, I knew what my father was trying to do, but I didn't believe him, and I knew that if I persisted, he would get angry and I didn't want that – so I backed down. But the silent suffering and misguided emotions inside me continued, and I felt secretly angry for years that I was not taken seriously by anyone that day – and it felt like an injustice was committed against me by a person who was automatically acquitted. I felt this issue would never be reconciled, or even properly addressed – and I was right.

Chapter Four:
Questions I Had As A Teen Resulting In Lessons I Learned As An Adult

The reality of racism might not dawn on you as a Visual Minority until you are in your teenage years. In the words of Dax, *"Remember when we were kids and didn't see color, and when we played in kindergarten and I called you my brother. Then we grew up, and they taught us we should hate on each other."* This captures what the transition from a child into a teenager looks like. It is at that point that you begin to realize that something is not right. In this chapter, we will discuss certain questions I struggled with in my teens in the 1990s and attempted to answer as an adult.

Why are older White-presenting people (who are strangers) so interested and so comfortable in asking me to explain to them what my ethnic backgrounds are but seem uncomfortable or less willing to reciprocate their question?

The inequity around me became obvious when I noticed that White-presenting people found it easier to ask me questions relating to my ethnicities at different times and in different places, but things turn awry and sour if I am the one asking them the question. It became evident that many of these people assume that being White is obvious and no one in their right senses is meant to be asking them to explain the origins of their ethnicity. Many times, when I tried asking them to explain their ethnicity, it appeared to me they may have felt insulted and embarrassed. Their expressions told me they felt I was being rude. Only a few were able to realize what I was trying to let them see.

Some of them realized that the question was uncomfortable and ridiculous when I put them in my shoes, and they apologized. However, these situations are exceptions rather than the status quo. Initially, I was enjoying how I was making the White-presenting people that asked me about my ethnicity uncomfortable by asking them to explain theirs. However, it became sickening at some point because almost every situation ended the same way. So, it became obvious to me that I was fighting a battle that had begun long before I was born. As an adult, I understood that the reason for this discomfort White-presenting people experience when a Visual Minority asks *them* about their ethnicity is that they feel it is obvious unless a person wants to be mischievous. It is terrible that we got to this point when two people living in the same nation have the same nationality but are treated as though they have different rights. Sports help us to forget the disparity once in a while, but sometimes it rears its ugly head all over again.

Why am I so uncomfortable answering ethnic-origin questions from White-presenting people but not from Visual Minority people?

Another reality that was puzzling is that, unlike when White-presenting people ask me about my ethnicity, I don't feel uncomfortable when Visual Minority people ask the same question. It dawned on me that when White-presenting people ask me to explain my ethnicity, I feel like a boss is interviewing me. I am under pressure and careful not to say something wrong. I knew that this feeling was not right but could not explain it to myself. On the other hand, when people from minority ethnic groups ask me ethnic-related questions, I see them as people trying to understand something they don't know. I provide answers with ease like a person talking to a friend or like a teacher trying to educate a child.

Even when I decide to ask them questions about their ethnicity, there is nothing mischievous about it. I ask them so that they can feel that I am interested in knowing them better or because I want to understand certain things about their culture. Still, I knew that something was not right. It became obvious that some people assume that they are superior to me because of their race. It is still as shocking today as it was when I realized it the first time. I could not understand why I was feeling like a second-class citizen in my country. I started asking probing questions from the people I felt could help but no one was able to provide satisfying answers. I didn't want answers based on sentiments but based on facts. It was this desire that prompted me to start digging into the past to understand the present situation. As an adult, my findings made me realize that this discomfort stemmed from historical slavery.

Why is it that wherever I go, no one looks like me? Why does that bother me?

It is never a comfortable feeling when you realize that you rarely see people that look like you when you move around. It puts pressure on you to question your identity, especially when these people don't treat you the same way they treat others. It makes you want to go back home and ask your parents certain questions. This was the situation I found myself in, in my early teens and early 1990s. I started battling an identity crisis. Of course, it is natural that we begin to define who we are and the kind of person we want to be at that stage of life. Still, it is more complex as a mixed Black and White teen, born in the late 1970s. Apart from the fact that you are thinking about the best career path for yourself and other such decisions, you also have to battle who you are because of the color of your skin.

What do I do with this reality staring me in the face, reminding me that I am different? It wasn't meant to be this bad. It would not have mattered much that I looked different if the people around me didn't treat me differently. The color of my skin would not have made any difference if I didn't have to try too hard to earn the acceptance of the people around me. It was hard to comprehend why someone else is treated with love and respect while I get the disdain for doing nothing wrong apart from the fact that I present as a minority. Each distasteful experience reminded me that I was different. As an adult, I realized that the reason no one looks like

64

me is the fact that I belonged to the mixed minority race in my nation.

Why do I feel that no matter how hard I work, I can't get a break as easily or as consistently as my White friends and White family?

It's the dream of everyone to get to that point in their lives when they will retire and enjoy their legacy and success. Even before then, we all want to have periods when we take a break and have marvelous vacations to some of the most exciting locations in the world. I think about things like this too but as a teenager, I was worried that I might never be able to do these things as effortlessly as my White friends and White family. I often secretly wondered why things have to be different just because I present as an Unidentifiable Visual Minority. I had genuine reasons to be concerned because I noticed a trend among the older people around me.

I noticed the disproportionate ratio of White-presenting people around me that were able to take advantage of career opportunities in comparison to the Visual Minority adults I know. I was worried that I might end up like the Visual Minority people I know who work multiple jobs just to cater to the needs of their families. I didn't want my life to be all about working without being able to have a flexible schedule due to the odds that I felt were stacked against me. I felt powerless to change the trend at a tender age and this was frustrating. It reduced my zeal and desire to want to give it my all because I felt that nothing I did was ever going to be enough. They say you should join them if you cannot beat them. In my case,

I felt I couldn't do either. I can't beat them, and I can't join them because I felt I would never be fully accepted.

As an adult, I understood that the disproportionate wealth gap between the majority and minority race was responsible for the difference between how White-presenting people and Visual Minority people could capitalize on a successful career opportunity.

Why do I feel I can't talk about my inequity experiences with anyone without feeling misunderstood and sometimes dismissed by my White father and other White-presenting people?

No matter how terrible an experience is, you will feel better when you have someone you can share it with, who would understand you. It gets worse when you just have to bottle it up because you feel that there is no point in telling anyone. After all, they wouldn't understand you. This was my dilemma. It was obvious to me that I was not getting the kind of treatment my White-presenting friends and White-presenting family got but no one understood me. Several times when I tried to have a conversation with my White father about my experiences, he would dismiss it and tell me to ignore those silly people that were stupid enough to disregard me because of my ethnicity.

Indeed, as always, there was wisdom in his words. I should just ignore what I see and act like it is nothing. However, it was easier said than done. I felt our society shouldn't be like that. We cannot keep telling people who are victims of racism to ignore the stupid people who perpetrate this act. Rather, we should be more proactive and deliberate about putting measures in place that will stamp out this wrong behavior. Victims shouldn't just deal with it. Besides, it is not everyone that has the mental strength to handle such treatments. As earlier stated, racial discrimination can lead to depression, even suicide. So, we shouldn't just offer coping mechanisms to the victims. We should be more concerned about eradicating these unacceptable actions from our society.

As an adult, I realized that many White-presenting people don't see racism as a serious problem and that is why they are quick to dismiss it.

Why is my entire White-presenting family wealthier and better educated than my Visual Minority family?

I have always been an observant person, and I put this skill to good use a lot. One of the things I observed in my teenage years is that my White family was wealthier and better educated than my Visual Minority family. It gave me reasons for concern. Could it be that my Visual Minority family didn't value education, or they just couldn't afford it? Was it because they didn't get the same opportunities that were available to my White-presenting family? I wanted answers to these questions so that I could know what to expect as I grew older. I didn't want to end up like my less educated Visual Minority family, but would I have what it takes to make that choice? Would 'working hard' be enough to achieve my dreams alone?

Will I have to work harder than my White-presenting family to get close to the level of success they have? I wanted to know what I was up against. I didn't want to be at a disadvantage in life. I wanted to grow up with the clear understanding that I could do anything I wanted to and achieve any dream I desired if I worked hard and gave it my all. Could it be that my Visual Minority family also wanted the same dream but couldn't achieve it because of the odds that were stacked against them? I wanted to know but I couldn't get satisfactory answers to these questions at that point in my life. I hoped to have better answers to these questions as I grew older, and I did.

My findings as an adult made me realize that it is the inequality in opportunities that have led to the reason White-presenting families are generally wealthier than Visual Minority families.

Am I a Visual Minority or am I White-presenting? Does it matter? If so, do I get a choice regarding how to identify? And what do people see when they look at me? - And is what other people see when they look at me, important somehow?

My identity crisis went on for a while. I was accepted by my White-presenting family, and it was meant to be enough for me, but it wasn't. Nothing could change the fact that I didn't look like them and some people out there usually reminded me of that fact whenever they could. I started getting concerned about what people think when they look at me. It is easier to know what some people think about me because they tell me. I had people that cared for me and respected me regardless of my ethnicity but some people didn't know me well, and they would try to make me feel bad about my mixed ethnicity.

My curiosity to know what others thought of me began to matter more than it used to. Of course, my best option was ignoring all the noise and focusing my energy on other more productive things. However, I could not because encounters with racially ignorant folks kept reminding me that there are people in my society that think less of me because of the color of my skin and because they could not classify me as a minority by looking at me. Once in a while, I would catch a person looking at me oddly and the process would start all over again. The desire to know what the person was thinking of me would come again and it is often uncontrollable for me to try to analyze the situation.

As an adult, I learned that I could not control the misguided judgements of others, but I could control the quality of how I respond to those misguided judgements, and never ignore how it makes me feel.

Why are 99% of my school teachers White-presenting? How do my teachers see me? Does it affect my grades? If so, what could I do about it?

Another question I battled in my early years was how the fact that I present as an Unidentifiable Visual Minority could affect my grades. It was natural for my mind to drift in this direction once in a while because 99% of my teachers were White-presenting. I understood the fact that the professional code of conduct would not permit them to express any explicit racial discriminatory words or actions against me. However, it still bothered me that some of them might not act the same when they are not within the confines of the school. I sometimes think that they might not like me but just pretend to cover it up because of the exemplary conduct that is expected of them as teachers.

What if some of my White-presenting teachers don't like me and that is the reason I didn't do well in some subjects. Sometimes it was quite difficult to believe that my grades were products of my efforts. There are days when I wonder if I had not had bad grades in a subject because my teacher was White-presenting, and I was an Unidentifiable Visual Minority. After all, some of the racially ignorant people in society could have been teachers. If they were in that position, I was convinced that they might manipulate the results to ensure that Visual Minority kids didn't do better than White-presenting kids. I wondered why the school didn't employ more Visual Minority teachers. Was it because they were not qualified, or they just didn't get the opportunity because of their skin color?

As an adult, I realized that at that time, systemic racism may have played an unseen role in the selection criteria of school teachers and this may have indirectly affected my grades in some ways (depending on which teacher was doing the grading).

Could the color of my skin interfere with me achieving success in the future as an adult?

The questions I asked myself regarding the link between the ethnicity of my teachers and my grades, often cascade into the link between my ethnicity and my success as an adult. If my ethnicity affected my grades, then it would affect my chances of achieving success as an adult. So, I needed to be sure that the color of my skin did not affect my grades. If the schools are not employing Visual Minority teachers and the hospitals are not employing Visual Minority doctors, then I would be in trouble when I grow older. Therefore, it was crucial at that point in my life that I am convinced that my race had nothing to do with my grades because if it did, then I had reason to be worried about my future.

Nothing could satisfy my curiosity. I needed to be sure that my mixed race would have nothing to do with my chances of getting to the pinnacle of my career. I needed to be certain that I would not be denied my dream job because of my skin color in the future. Also, I wanted to be sure that I would not be denied the promotion or pay raise I deserve when I got my dream job just because I am an Unidentifiable Visual Minority. I didn't know how at that point, but I knew that I needed to get answers as soon as possible.

My discovery as an adult has made me realize that my skin color would affect my chances of success, without a doubt, unless things change drastically.

Why can't I stop asking these questions of myself?

The most confusing of all the questions I asked myself as a teenager is the reason I couldn't stop asking myself all these questions regarding my mixed ethnicity. Why can't I just stop asking myself these questions? There were some days when I would deliberately try to focus on other things in life and try to enjoy myself more. Still, I am aware that I am a hair-trigger away from moving around that circle again. Why couldn't these questions go away? Does every Mixed Kid out there have the same issues? Do they also think about all these things or was I just a different type of person? Could it be that my curiosity and observational skills are becoming a curse?

Would these questions go away when I grow older or I will have to spend the rest of my life battling them? I wished I had some kind of magical power that would make all these questions vanish. Although I wanted to stop filling my mind with these kinds of thoughts, I knew that it was practically impossible. I understood that the reason these questions didn't go away was that my skin tone would not change. How am I supposed to deny what was right before me? Nothing was changing. So, there was no way I could ignore the trends that kept popping up. Things would have to change before I would be able to take these thoughts out of my mind.

As an adult, I realized that I couldn't stop asking myself these questions because several experiences kept reminding me about them, but I knew there was no meaningful answer.

Chapter Five:
Basic Inequity Education

Denying the fact that inequity exists in the world today is either an attempt to be dishonest or a grave situation where the person in question is oblivious and ignorant about the happenings in his or her environment. In this chapter, we will explore basic terms that will be helpful in understanding inequity and related concepts.

Inequality vs Inequity

We must distinguish between inequity and inequality as we begin this journey. Note that inequity is not the same as inequality, even though they are often used interchangeably. Inequality is inevitable while inequity is avoidable. Inequality is an uneven distribution of resources due to certain factors such as age, educational level, or political status. For example, a doctor gets more pay than a janitor in the hospital. This is inequality and it is not necessarily wrong. Also, an adult likely gets more food in the home than a child. This is inequality, and as I mentioned earlier, it is unavoidable.

Inequality is excusable because, in the case of a doctor and a cleaner, even though they are both doing something critical, one is more skills-sensitive than the other. Besides, it does not require years of training and specialization to be a cleaner. On the other hand, the doctor will have to go through years of training that will demand a lot of money before he or she can be qualified to treat people. So, it is understandable that the salary of a doctor is far above what the janitor earns. In the same way, in a family, the amount of food required by an adult to be able to function and carry out his or her daily tasks is far greater than is required by a child. Therefore, it will not be out of place for an adult in a family to get more food than a child.

Based on the examples above, I believe you have a good idea of what I mean by saying that inequality is unavoidable. It is necessary for various aspects of life. Sometimes, countries use it in the allocation of budgets. For example, a state that contributes more to the GDP of a nation might get more from the federal government allocation than states that contribute less. So, there are instances when inequality is a form of meritocracy. There are usually justifiable reasons for inequalities. When there is inequality, the path for those that didn't get the same treatment knows what to do to change the narrative. However, the same cannot be said about inequity.

For example, the janitor knows that if he gets educated and acquires the same educational qualification as the doctor, he will also get the same pay. The child knows that he will get the same quantity of food when he grows older. The states also know that they will get the same amount of allocation when they contribute more to the GDP of the nation.

On the other hand, inequity is the deliberate attempt to deny a person of what is due to him or her due to sentiments such as age, gender, race, or religion. For example, if a White-presenting doctor gets more pay than a Visual Minority doctor, this is inequity. In the same way, if a Christian doctor gets more pay than a Muslim doctor, this is inequity. Therefore, what we are dealing with in this book is inequity. To be precise, we are discussing racial inequity. When inequity is the problem, there is no clear path to turn things around. There is nothing the Visual Minority doctor can do to get the same pay as the White-presenting doctor because he cannot change the color of his skin. In the same way, there is nothing the Muslim doctor can do to get the same pay as the Christian doctor unless he changes his religious allegiance.

I believe that you can see why inequity is so frustrating, from these illustrations. It will make you strive harder to get the same recognition and respect as another person just because of the color of your skin. It is painful and frustrating because you get humiliated and disrespected for nothing apart from the stereotype that has been assumed against your race. I will try, as much as possible, not to get too emotional throughout this book, but you can trust me to be honest when necessary. There are indeed Visual Minority people that have acted in wrong ways and there are those that still do things that are unacceptable in society. However, this is not the basis to judge every Visual Minority person wrongly. Some White-presenting people have been found doing things they ought not to do. So, should every White-presenting person be called a criminal just because there are White-presenting people that have committed crimes and are in prison?

This is what is ridiculous about racial inequity. Racists assume that everyone from a particular race is rude and aggressive just because they have met certain people from that race that have been rude and acted aggressively towards them. The physical and emotional damages that victims of racial maltreatment have gotten as a result of this unacceptable stereotype, cannot be quantified. It is never a good situation to find yourself in when you know that you are not truly accepted, and you are just one mistake away from being reminded about your skin color. It is said that even Visual Minority celebrities who have achieved fame and success in music, football, and other career paths, still get this unacceptable treatment.

In the recently concluded Euro 2020, Bukayo Saka, Marcus Rashford, and Jando Sancho were subjected to racial slurs online because they missed penalties that led to the loss of the English football team against Italy. These guys play for Manchester United and Arsenal, two of the best teams in England. Still, it did not stop insensitive people from reminding them that they are Visual Minorities after they, unfortunately, missed the decisive penalties.

Difference Between Race, Culture, And Ethnicity

Just like equity and equality, race, culture, and ethnicity are also often used interchangeably. Meanwhile, they don't mean the same thing. They are all used for classifying people into certain groups based on certain shared characteristics but the parameters they use are not the same. Knowing the meaning of each of them will help to paint a clearer picture regarding their differences. Based on this, we will start by explaining and defining each one to spell out the marked differences between these two often interchanged words.

Race refers to a classification of people based on geographic ancestry, physical appearances, and heritable characteristics. On the other hand, culture refers to the classification of people based on their shared values and beliefs. It often entails the language, livelihoods, region, religion, and spirituality of a particular set of people. Meanwhile, ethnicity is a sense of peoplehood. It is the sense of similarity people have because they share certain characteristics that are common to them such as skin color, dialect, religion, and customs.

Ethnicity is a combination of race and culture. In other words, people that belong to the same ethnic group share similar culture and they belong to the same race. So, in the context of this discussion, we will focus more on distinguishing between a race and a culture because it is possible that people belong to the same race but don't share a similar culture. The first thing that can be observed between race and culture is that race is inherited while culture is learned. In other words, you can choose your culture, but you cannot choose your race. This point is cogent and will be very useful as we continue to dive deeper into this conversation.

The fact that you don't get to choose your race is one of the reasons it is ridiculous to treat people with disrespect or prevent them from enjoying certain rights. People should earn respect based on merit and not because they are White-presenting or Visual Minorities. A race is acquired through the transfer of genes from the parents to the offspring. So, if your parents are Caucasians, it is natural that you will be White. In the same way, if your parents are Visual Minorities, you will have the same traits. It will be an abnormality of the highest order to see Visual Minority parents give birth to Caucasian kids.

Even when it is explained to be a product of recessive genes, it will still be absurd. So, you don't get to choose to be Asian, African, or Caucasian. On the other hand, culture is learned. It depends on where you grow up and what you learn from your family and the society you find yourself in. If your parents are Muslims, you likely turn out to be a Muslim unless you choose otherwise when you are older. The same can be said about people whose parents are Christians. Also, if your parents are medical doctors, the chances are very high that you choose that path.

If you grow up in an area close to the sea where most people are fishermen, your dream would likely be to become one of the greatest fishermen ever. This is the reason John Locke, an English philosopher, referred to the mind of a child at birth as **tabula rasa**. In other words, he believed that the human mind at the state of birth is like a clean slate that has nothing written in it. I agree with this concept too. So, your culture was written on this clean slate of yours over time.

One of the common traits of culture and race is that they both involve discrimination. People can label you and call you unacceptable names because of your race. This is also applicable to culture. You might get mocking remarks because you practice Judaism, Christianity, or Islam. You might also be discriminated against if you don't believe in God by people who do. Even when people share similar cultures and religions, there are still sects and divisions who believe certain sets of people are not doing things the right way. Of course, you don't have to share the beliefs and cultures of others, but you shouldn't disrespect them because of that.

We live in a world where it is difficult to find people who respect others regardless of their race, religion, or culture. It is understandable if people are criticized because of their culture because they choose to adopt and live by it, but you don't get to make that decision when it comes to your race. You can leave a region to another place and adopt a new way of life that is different from how you grew up. However, your race is permanent. There is nothing you can do about it.

Sadly, one of the cultures some people learned and developed is racism. You inherited your race, but racism is learned. People learn to be racist due to the kind of parents they have and the kind of people they have around them. They have been told certain things about other races that have given them the idea that their race is superior to others. How can something you never get to choose make you inferior or superior to others? It is quite ridiculous that some people have this mindset, to say the least.

The good news is that racism can be unlearned because it was learned. You can choose to have a different view and choose to respect others who are not from your race, even if you grew up around people who treated people from other races as trash. In a beautiful piece by American rapper, Dax, called "Black Lives Matter," he said, "Nobody's born racist, man; it's something you learn; deep-rooted in your brain from the day of your birth." It is this beacon of hope that has encouraged me to keep speaking and writing against racism over the years. If racism can be unlearned, then we can all contribute our quota towards educating our society to see things the right way and learn to honor others, regardless of their race or culture.

Language: 3 Racial Positions

Before we draw the curtain on this chapter, we will explore the three racial positions people hold, which will be used in the subsequent chapters. The three racial positions are:

- Racially ignorant

- Racially neutral

- Anti-racist

Racially Ignorant

These are people who are not aware of the pain that denigrating words, actions, or beliefs may inadvertently cause another culture or race due to a lack of consequential thinking. When such people speak to others using racial slurs, they think they are just having fun or just expressing themselves. Unknown to them, they are hurting others in ways they are not aware of. They cannot understand the anguish they put others through by speaking or acting in ways that remind others of the fact that they are not welcome due to their race or culture. In some cases, they grew up around people who act in such ways towards others and they have come to see it as a way of life. They cannot see anything wrong with what they are doing.

For people in this category, they will never stop acting this way until they get a dose of their medicine. They may never understand the consequences of their actions until they are treated that way or their actions lead to the death of some people. According to a study by the University of Houston, there is a link between racial discrimination and suicidal ideation. The study showed that perceived racial discrimination serves as a sufficiently painful experience to make the American adults overcome their inherent fear of death and empower them to harm themselves. How would you feel when you realize that your actions have directly or indirectly led to the death of another person? It doesn't have to get that far before you realize that your actions are causing pain to others.

Racially Neutral

The people in this category have passive beliefs, values, observations, and thoughts that acknowledge the existence of racism and advocate the separation from the activity of racism but do not actively interfere with or question the existence of racism or attempt to self-educate the oppressive effects of racist behaviors, racist beliefs, and racist communication. Unlike the first set of people, racially neutral individuals do not inflict pain on others through their actions or words. However, they are not interested in doing anything significant to end racism. Just like the first group, one of the reasons people are racially neutral is that they cannot relate to the pain and anguish experienced by people who are victims of racism.

Indeed, racially neutral people are not causing harm to others, but their inactions are part of the reasons racism will never be eradicated. In "Black Lives Matter," Dax said something very crucial that racially neutral people should pay attention to. He said, "Everybody has a voice, don't you dare be silent. If you say nothing, you are an accessory to violence." In other words, the fact that you are saying nothing and doing nothing is an indirect way of saying yes to racism. If your daughter comes home and says that she has been hanging out with some guys recently and has been smoking and abusing alcohol, saying nothing is an indirect way of saying that you approve of the behavior.

Dax has something to say to you:

"Spread love, show love, let's get rid of this curse; don't wait for anyone to act, man, you go first."

Anti-racist

Anti-racists leverage active and thoughtful communication that tactfully and intentionally interferes with racist activity of any kind or attempts to advocate racist education to the racially neutral and the racially ignorant. What we need to end the overdue stay of racism in our society are anti-racists. We need more men and women from both sides of the divide to show their disgust toward racism and educate others to begin to take giant strides toward stamping out this menace. Nothing will change until we have more of such people. In the words of Dax:

"Change is what we really need. Cut me open, cut you open, red's the color, every human being bleeds. Let's come together, cops, citizens, and in between, and rally for the rights of everybody in humanity. Black, blue, white, green, playing for the same team."

Visual Minority people shouldn't be the only people trying to eliminate racism in our society. I know that every person who presents as White is not racist. Still, you cannot afford to be silent during these sensitive times. Staying silent and doing nothing because you are not a victim of racism is the reason we have not achieved monumental changes in the bid to end racism. So, it is time for every good cop to speak out to show that police brutality is the action of some bad cops. It is time for every White-presenting person against racism to speak out so that others will learn.

Chapter Six:
What Could Be Inspiring Racism In Canada And The United States?

We will continue this journey by looking at the possible reason racism continues to thrive in Canada and the United States. Racism could not have been created by any single event, but something went wrong somewhere. Unfortunately, we have not been able to fix it. So, in this chapter, we will explore the factors sustaining racism so that we would know how to retrace our steps and perhaps consider setting things right.

What Perpetuates Racism?

From my perspective, below are some of the things that perpetuate racism:

Misdirected Anger

When I was 10, I asked my father why the Israelis and Arabs still don't get along. Why don't they just stop fighting? My father got so angry as a result of me asking. He yelled at me saying: did you know that the Arabs want to push the Jews into the sea?! I said, no, and I'm glad no one I know wants to do that to me.

A few years later, I brought that angry instance up to a psychologist my father and I were seeing. I said it made me feel uncomfortable. The psychologist said, "Maybe you shouldn't discuss this anymore and see that new movie together 'Scent of A Woman' with Al Pacino." My father and I saw the movie, and afterwards, I still felt awkward.

From that point, I associated punishment with racial dialogue, and I never felt comfortable with discussing racial inequity with my father again. I couldn't understand why he was so angry instead of being willing to explain. I am convinced that this misdirected anger is one of the reasons racism has continued to thrive in our society. Instead of channeling our energy towards weakening systemic racism, and anyone who would perpetrate this act, we are sometimes angry about the fact that some were brave enough to bring up the issue so that it can be addressed.

Lack Of Consequential Thinking Before Speaking And Acting

Consequential thinking is when you have an understanding of the gravity of what you are about to do, before doing it. Sadly, many people that perpetuate racism don't have this manner of thinking. They have no idea that their words and actions are going to cause pain to others. Many of these people never get to understand what they are doing to others until something disastrous, such as a loss of life, happens.

Unconscious Ignorance Stemming From Not Having Visual Minority Friends

One of the reasons racists lack consequential thinking before speaking and acting is that they don't have BIPOC friends. When the people you care about are open to you about how they feel about your actions, it might give you a reason to rethink the impact of what you do to them. For example, it is not likely that White-presenting people that have Visual Minority friends will use racial slurs because they understand that it hurts when they use such words against their friends.

Never Realizing That Racism Is A Problem

This happens most times because it doesn't painfully affect people who visually present as White. If there's no pain, it's easy to dismiss, forget, minimize, and downplay it. So, unless more White-presenting people begin to understand the pain that Visual Minority people and other people belonging to minority races experience daily due to racial discrimination, we might not be close to ending this problem any time soon. Empathy is needed to garner more support and make racists rethink their actions. Like I said earlier, racism is learned and therefore can be unlearned. Putting others in our shoes can help us to make tremendous progress in this regard.

Caring More About Non-Racist Optics Than Confronting The Problem Of Racism

Many see racism as a controversial topic. Indeed, it is because it often stirs emotions. Still, we cannot pretend it does not exist. The fact that it is not a topic many people like to discuss, doesn't change the fact that it is a crucial issue pervading our society that is making many suffer in silence. Many feel that confronting the problem seems much larger than anticipated.

A Lot Of Modern-Day Racism Is Quiet And Hidden From Sight

The truth is that things are slightly different in our days because, unlike in the past, there seems to be a consensus that racism is unacceptable social behavior. Still, this doesn't mean that racism is no more. Many feel that it has reduced drastically because a lot of modern-day racism is quiet and hidden from sight to avoid social accountability and guilt. On rare occasions when certain situations get out of hand, it reminds us all that racism has not gone away but has become a silent operator, still making many shed tears.

Confusing Anti-Racism With Neutral Racism

One of the reasons many don't want to discuss racism is because they confuse anti-racism with neutral racism. In other words, they assume the fact that many people are indifferent to racism means that we have many people that are willing to speak up against racism, correct, and educate others about this wrong action. If things are going to change, we need more neutral racists to become anti-racists.

Could Some People Not Know They Could Be Racist?

Some people think that the fact that they have Visual Minority people as their colleagues, employees, and neighbors means that they are not racist. Unknown to them, they could be ignorantly or passively racist. In the case of White-presenting people, the reason they never knew is that there is no way for White-presenting people to experience oppressive racism on any level. If you are White-presenting, you might need to consciously analyze how you view Visual Minority people. Do you believe that they are equal when compared to White-presenting people? It is not enough to have Minority employees and colleagues; it is how you rate them when compared with White-presenting people that determine whether you are racist or not.

Many Racists Don't Know How To Change

Interestingly, many racists who, embarrassingly, know they are racists, either want to change but don't know how, or maybe uncomfortable with the thought of losing their privilege/entitlement if they do change into behaving anti-racist. Also, some racist people don't believe there's a problem at all because they are not oppressed and simply don't feel the pain of inequity (which is arguably the source of their racist ignorance).

For White-presenting people that realize that they are racists and want to change, they may be able to find plausible ways to do that as we continue this journey. However, it is difficult to help people who know that they are racists but don't want to change because they don't want to lose some of the social privileges and entitlements they enjoy because they are White-presenting.

A Lack Of Educational Resources

One of the reasons there is a lack of educational resources on racism is that the subject of anti-racism is not taken seriously by the dominant race (White-presenting people) that created and largely controls the history/education system (among every other North American system as a result of British colonialism). The education system would have been the best way to educate people about this issue so that we can produce sensitive adults who see racism as wrong behavior. However, since there is a lack of emphasis on this wrong attitude in the early phase of life, as well as in school, some White-presenting people never get to know that it is not proper to avoid accepting the Visual Minority people as equals solely based on their skin color.

Removal Of Racist Education From History Books

Substituting racist education from history books for listening to Visual Minority people's stories and insights (and taking those stories and insights as seriously as their own opinions) is another reason racism has not gone away.

Optimism On Being Heard

As I grew older, I started developing optimism that racism can end someday. However, this was not the case when I was younger. As a kid, how could I explain to myself why my White family seems unknowingly racially ignorant? And why does the thought of talking about it make me feel there's no point in trying? I mean, trying to explain what pain feels like to someone who's never felt pain before felt pointless to me. Besides, some of the few moments that I tried to start a discussion with my White-presenting father and other people around me, didn't lead to positive endings.

So, at some point in my youth, I convinced myself that there is no point in trying again. I thought, how could I possibly turn things around when the people that are supposed to listen to me, are not interested in discussing the topic and take me seriously? Long before the Black Lives Matter Movement began, I started to get more curious in engaging people regarding racial inequity and just having peaceful conversations (starting with my Visual Minority mother). It felt like a drop in the ocean at that point, but I was optimistic that my little efforts might amount to something someday. At least, unlike when I was a kid, I made up my mind not to give up again on having these peaceful but honest chats.

Sometimes, questions would run through my mind. What would happen if nothing changed after I had tried to have peaceful but honest interactions about racism? Would it cost me my relationships? Still, it didn't deter me. I told myself I have nothing to lose. If I don't do anything, racism might continue in my tiny world, but if I do start sharing, at least, there is a chance that things might change for the better in my relationships with family and friends. When the Black Lives Matter movement began, I was really glad because it gave me the confidence knowing that there are other people out there that may feel the way I do.

Of course, I have always known that many people are not racist, but they have been too silent. It is their silence and lackadaisical attitude to the racism that has contributed to the existence of this issue. So, I was really happy to see that some White-presenting people are coming out to have conversations and listen to the personal stories and history of racism from Visual Minorities. It gave me a glimmer of hope that we might not be far from the early beginnings of a future society we want to nurture.

I felt we may be a bit closer to building that nation where minority races don't have to prepare to think about what to do or say when harassed or violated because of their ethnic appearance. It has boosted my morale and I am more determined than ever to do my part to build on the momentum that has been gathered so far. But the onus is on all of us to keep the fire burning so that we can march on to victory.

Chapter Seven:
White Privilege And Entitlement

To me, White privilege and White entitlement are some of the things that scream racism. Sadly, many people are not willing to let them go or acknowledge their existence, which has contributed significantly to the inability to curb racism in our society. In this chapter, we will explore the meaning of White privilege and White entitlement and how they affect the nature of or perpetuate racism.

What is White Privilege?

White privilege refers to the opportunities that are available to a person because they visually present as White, which others do not enjoy because of their Visual Minority appearance. When you have White privilege, your skin color won't hold you back from being given a chance to work hard to achieve success or be distracted by the pain of not being given a chance to work hard and achieve success readily. White-presenting people get to look away and forget racist issues, racist perceptions, and racist crimes if they choose. It is vital to note that White privilege doesn't mean you don't work hard or haven't had a tough life.

You can still be White-presenting and have a tough life because of various circumstances. Sometimes, you might struggle because of the choices you made. For example, a White-presenting person might choose to abuse drugs until he or she is addicted. He or she will face the consequences of this choice. In the same way, a White-presenting person can choose to live a life of crime that can lead to being prosecuted and imprisoned. So, White privilege does not guarantee a good life. However, it gives a White-presenting person an undue advantage that makes it easier to achieve success than a Visual Minority. A person who presents as White will never be held back on the road to success because of their skin color.

Of course, it is still possible for a Visual Minority person to be more successful than a White-presenting person. Still, it requires more mental strength because you will battle against systemic racism and biased treatment. In other words, apart from the fact that you will face regular challenges that are common to every other person to make the right decisions, you also have to face the fear of being discriminated against because of your race. You will face insensitive people who feel that you don't deserve to be successful and might deny you the same opportunities that are readily available to others, especially White-presenting people.

There are situations where it may be obvious to you as a Visual Minority person that you are being denied the opportunity to show what you can do and the value you can add because of your race. However, in some cases, it is not explicit. In it all, you have more factors that can make you unable to achieve your dreams, unlike a White-presenting person. In a dog-eat-dog society, many White-presenting people may unconsciously feel they cannot give up their social privileges. They like the fact that sometimes they get access to certain opportunities with less effort. So, it is easier for a White-presenting person to choose to be racially neutral because he or she does not get to experience the same treatments meted out to Visual Minority people.

Some White-presenting people are not aware that they are enjoying certain privileges that are not available to Visual Minority people. It is this lack of awareness or lack of observation that makes some of them racially ignorant or racially neutral. They might not be able to relate to it and understand when a Visual Minority person is complaining about racial inequity. The Visual Minority person might be mistaken for someone giving excuses, or too sensitive. The fact that some Visual Minority people are successful does not mean that all opportunities are equal.

White Entitlement

White privilege is similar to White entitlement, but they are not the same. Sometimes, White privilege leads to White entitlement. White entitlement refers to the access given to White-presenting people to enter various places with less scrutiny. For example, unless you appear destitute, White-presenting people can go anywhere (that's allowed by law) and not be inappropriately watched, questioned, or judged by other White-presenting people. It's the ability to live without having to consciously consider any social consequences whatsoever because invisible inequality is on the side of the White-presenting people. For example, at the airport, I have to shave my face and remove my hat so that I will look less racially threatening to passengers and security while standing in line. I've tested this theory, and unfortunately, the optics of it all are real.

I have to do this to ensure that I am less likely to be profiled. On the other hand, I've seen White-presenting people in line ahead of me with beards and ball caps on without ever having to think about altering their appearance to pass through security without being stopped for the way they look. White entitlement is a form of systemic racism. No signal or sign says that Visual Minority people have to be checked especially, unlike their White-presenting counterparts. In the same way, no legislation says this. Still, it is the reality that many Visual Minority people must face.

I have noticed, many White-presenting people cannot come to terms with the fact that they enjoy White entitlement. Unknown to many of them, they have an invisible immunity that makes them be perceived as less threatening than a Visual Minority. The high level of moral standard a Visual Minority has to adhere to before he or she can be considered less threatening cannot be compared to what is expected of a White-presenting person. Certain characteristics that send alarm bells to the minds of security agents do not have the same impact when it comes to White-presenting people.

Why should I be afraid of leaving my face unshaved or wearing a hat when approaching a security agent, but a White-presenting person does not have to worry about such things? You are more likely to be profiled and placed under surveillance as a Visual Minority than as a White-presenting person. So, the playing field is not level in this area. Have there been Visual Minority people that have been criminals because they hurt others? Yes. Have there been Visual Minority people that have been prosecuted for perpetrating injurious acts? Yes. However, the same can also be said about White-presenting people.

If you were to visit our prisons, you'd quickly see that it is not only Visual Minority people that are there. This shows that criminality has nothing to do with race. Hurting others is a choice that can be made by anyone regardless of the color of their skin. So, the same measures should be used when profiling a White-presenting person and a Visual Minority. We should be dealing with people based on their merits in society. A Visual Minority man with a beard is not more likely to commit crimes than a White-presenting man with a beard.

Why Is The Issue Not Addressed?

Although White privilege and White entitlement pervade our society, it is surprising that there are no concerted efforts to address these issues. There are some reasons for this lackadaisical attitude towards these problems. One of them is that they are not considered as serious topics that need urgent attention. Issues that affect everyone in society such as insecurity, healthcare, employment, and housing often enjoy urgent attention because they are common problems. Interestingly, even when it comes to these social issues, they affect people that belong to minority races more than White-presenting people.

For example, according to a report by Public Health England in 2020, the chances of Covid-19 diagnosis were twice as high among Minority Presenting ethnic groups in comparison to their White counterparts. Meanwhile, the highest mortality rate was in areas with Visual Minority people living in more deprived places. The report showed that 4.5% of the English population is made up of people from the Visual Minority. Moreover, the National Health Service (NHS) workforce is made up of 21% of people from this community. Besides, it was observed that the first eleven doctors to die in the UK were from the Black, Asian, and Minority Ethnic (BAME) communities.

I don't want to believe that all of these are mere coincidences. The poverty rate among people of Visual Minority backgrounds is twice as high when compared to White-presenting people. However, people from the Visual Minority communities are more likely to be engaged in frontline roles than their White-presenting counterparts. This unacceptable and indiscriminate engagement of people from the Visual Minority communities during Covid-19 further shows the disturbing inequities in the UK health sector as an example. It simply reaffirmed the strong link between race, socioeconomic status, ethnicity, and health outcomes. The observed differences are represented by the unacceptable risks to Visual Minority staff within the NHS workspace, high racial predisposition to particular diseases, unequal distribution of resources, and the disproportionate engagement of Visual Minority communities. These inequalities require urgent and drastic attention to reduce or eliminate the damage to health and lives suffered by the Visual Minority communities.

It is said that this pattern of racial discrimination in the health sector is also prevalent in other areas in the UK, Canada, and the US. Many White-presenting people are not even aware that they are enjoying certain privileges that are not available to Visual Minority people. So, it is not surprising that there is no consensus among the people of these nations to speak out about their experiences with racism. Racism goes beyond using racial slurs or racially abusing people. It is rooted in the system as demonstrated by these stats during the pandemic. The Black Lives Matter movement has brought hope that perhaps something will change. However, the reality is that we are going to be patient and strategic to eventually make this topic easier to address.

Is There Black Privilege?

No. There are no social opportunities to benefit Visual Minority people exclusively. Nothing comes to mind when you try to analyze how you are at an advantage as a -presenting over a White-presenting person. Even the rate of being diagnosed with diseases does not favor Visual Minority people. For example, according to data from the former National Cancer Intelligence Network on lung and breast cancer, women of the -presenting ethnic group were more likely to be diagnosed with cancer in the last stage than White women. The report also showed that diagnosis of colorectal and lung cancer at the final stage was more prevalent among people of -presenting ethnic group origin than people from other ethnic groups.

In a recent review, evidence of ethnic inequalities in London was consolidated. NICE (National Institute for Health and Care Excellence), in 2013, discovered that the Visual Minority ethnic group is at a higher risk of type 2 diabetes than their White European counterparts, especially at a lower BMI.

Many have tried to explain this disparity among ethnic groups away by citing behavioral theories. These theories explain that the reason people from minority groups are experiencing health inequalities is that they engage in damaging behaviors that take their toll on their health. At face value, this explanation seems to suffice. Still, a more critical outlook will make it untenable. The differences in behavior could have been due to factors such as target marketing or the absence of opportunities to be engaged in more meaningful and morale-boosting activities. So, this explanation is too simplistic to explain the reason for ethnic-based health inequalities observed among the people living in London.

Even when it comes to housing, there are far more Visual Minority people living in areas that are likely to complicate their health conditions than White-presenting people. According to the Department for Work and Pensions (2015), 15% of the United Kingdom's population lives on a low income. Low income, in this context, refers to an income below 60% of the median national income. This statistic is not the same among ethnic groups. For example, only 14% of this population belongs to the White ethnic group. So, it is obvious that there is no such thing as Black privilege. A Visual Minority will have to strive harder than a White person to achieve success. Many have been able to do it but many are never able to break the barrier placed in the system against them because of the color of their skin.

How Do You Convince White-Presenting People That White Privilege Exists?

There is no doubt that removing racism from our society is not something that will happen overnight. The reality of the deep-rooted nature of the issue is enough to make you want to forget about it and get on with your life. This has been the way most Visual Minority people (which may include other minorities) have faced the situation. They see it as something that will not change. So, instead of choosing to complain, they have chosen to ignore

101

racism either as an action of an individual or what is embedded in the system. Many White-presenting people that are not racist also advise Visual Minority people this way.

I believe we cannot continue to accept racism as something that will never go away. We need to switch from that mindset that it is a problem that has come to stay, and whoever is a victim, should find ways to cope. We should never forget that there are people that might never be able to survive these kinds of abuses.

We need to start by letting White-presenting people understand that there is such a thing as White privilege and White entitlement. I am convinced that this will help more racially neutral White-presenting people to be more active about educating other White-presenting people to level the playing field. Through the tools of continued dialogue, protest when necessary, and racial education, we can start turning the tide. If White privilege and entitlement are things only known by Visual Minority people, we are not going to make any significant progress. No one will attempt to solve a problem when they don't believe that there is one. So, if only Visual Minority people are aware that they are not treated equally as their counterparts are, we cannot get enough support that will be needed to cause the kind of change we need in our society.

Just like many Visual Minority people, I am committed to speaking up for my race and letting anyone who cares to listen, know that all people are created equal. Still, I understand that nothing will change if we don't get more

White-presenting people involved in this battle. Racism has to be a problem that is recognized by most people. Beyond the recognition and acceptance by the majority, all hands must be on deck to stamp it out of our communities. I will not stop talking and trying to enlighten others about the dangers of a society that is unfair to certain people because of their race and I hope to have more White-presenting people on this train.

For My White Brothers and Sisters

In *White Boy*, Tom MacDonald spoke about the importance of realizing that all White-presenting people are not racist. He also spoke about not making White-presenting people feel responsible for something their ancestors did to Visual Minority people. This is the truth. It will be unfair to label all White-presenting people as racists because that is not the truth. For my White brothers and sisters, are you White? Or do you present as White? And how does that affect your privilege and entitlement? You don't have to be the victim before you stand against something wrong.

For example, you don't have to be a homeless person to stand for the rights of the homeless. In the same way, you don't have to be a woman to stand up for the rights of women in your community. So, the fact that you are not the victim of racism doesn't mean that you should not be concerned about it. If you are convinced that it is wrong, then it should be obvious to the people around you that you stand against it. Too many White-presenting people are sitting on the fence, and that is one of the major reasons we don't seem to be getting anywhere regarding the goal to end racism in our society. Your standpoint should be clear so that no one will assume that you are what you are not.

When a Visual Minority stands against racism, it is understandable because he or she is the victim of this unacceptable behavior. It might not gain the attention of people and the relevant authority. However, when White-presenting people stand against racism, it carries more weight. It will be obvious that he or she is not doing it because it is affecting him or her. Rather, the person is doing it because it is wrong and should be eradicated in our community. So, if you are a White-presenting person and you are reading this, stand up and speak out against racism if you believe it is inappropriate. Be more vocal and active to ensure that other people from your race don't look down on others because of the color of their skin.

We cannot go back to the past to undo all the wicked things White-presenting people did to Visual Minority people during the slave and colonial era. Yet, you can prove that you wouldn't have done the same if you were in their shoes by standing up for Visual Minority people in your community. The Black Lives Matter protest was so beautiful because of how people from various races, including White-presenting people, came together with one voice to speak against this social ill. It shouldn't be the peak; rather, it should be the beginning of a new dawn when White-presenting people, Visual Minorities, and other races see themselves as brothers and sisters, where an injury to one is perceived as an injury to all.

Chapter Eight:
What Encourages Racism

Before now, I mentioned the lack of consequential thinking before speaking and acting as one of the reasons people are racially ignorant. However, this is not the only reason. Meanwhile, it is crucial to understand why people racially abuse others and racially discriminate against others to be able to know how to handle the issue. So, in this chapter, I will highlight more of the things that encourage racist behavior.

Racial Unfamiliarity

If you're White-presenting, when was the last time you had Visual Minority people over for dinner in your home or had a conversation with a group of Visual Minority people? If you have, that's great. But many White-presenting people have never had reasons to do things together with Visual Minority people. Some of them have only seen the way the media projects Visual Minority people and what the people around them say about Visual Minorities. This can make them form their perception about Visual Minority people from the wrong source. Sadly, some of them have parents who have not been close to Visual Minority people too, who have wrong views.

Remember that the family is the first agent of socialization. Meanwhile, the parents are the first teachers of their children. So, if a White-presenting boy has been told by his parents that Visual Minority people are aggressive people who are too lazy to earn a living and lack the kind of talent to move America forward, the child will have this perception about this race. The boy might grow up into an adult with this same mindset and pass it on to his children. Many White-presenting people never get the chance to observe Visual Minority people at close quarters. They only view them from the eye lenses of their parents and media. Once the parents have ignorant prejudice against Visual Minority people, the chances are very high that the child will share the same opinion.

They might never have the opportunity to see Visual Minority people that have commendable traits, which can make them believe socially constructed stereotypes about these people. They might assume that every Visual Minority out there is aggressive and dangerous because they saw a hostile Visual Minority in a movie or paraded in the news as a criminal. There is a way such social construction of a race can be misleading to people who are not ready to make their findings of these individuals. There are indeed Visual Minority people out there that are not friendly and can hurt others if given the chance.

However, the same can be said about some White-presenting people. At some point, a colleague kept complaining that the people in his community were hostile and unfriendly to strangers. I could not understand why he kept saying that because I met some of the most hospitable people I know in this same community. So, I kept wondering why he kept thinking this way about people in that environment. One day, I got tired of his wrong perception of the people in that community. So, I took him to meet a family I had visited several times in that community.

This family welcomed him and spoke in a welcoming way to him. On our way home, I reminded him that he had been wrong to think that only hostile people live in that place. This is the issue sometimes. We use stereotypes that are based on questionable conjectures. I have met White-presenting people that are racists. Still, I know that all White-presenting people are not racists because some of my friends are White-presenting and they are nice people. So, for a change, deliberately start looking for Visual Minority people that have commendable behavior; you will find many of them.

Factions

A social psychology experiment called "Minimal Group Phenomenon" revealed that people develop feelings of responsibility and belonging towards members of the same group because they believe that being a part of the group demands cooperation and support for one another. When people are part of a group, they tend to display support for the members. There is nothing wrong with this. This is the same reason a Christian will likely help another Christian rather than a Muslim, who he considers not to be a part of his "group." This is the same reason people from the same family are likely to help each other in comparison with someone else from another family.

In some cases, some brothers might maltreat their younger ones. However, if an outsider should do the same things they did to their siblings, they would try to defend them. They want the outsider to know that they have an emotional connection to their siblings. So, the fact that someone belongs to the same group doesn't guarantee that people from that group wouldn't do things that might hurt him or her. Visual Minority people cheat one another and White-presenting people do the same. However, if a White-presenting person hurts a Visual Minority, it is not likely that he feels as guilty as when he does the same to a White person. He or she might not even be remorseful at all if he or she is racially ignorant.

As I said, there is nothing wrong with the fact that you display support and care for a person that belongs to a class of people you consider as your group. However, the issue is that people often display hostility toward people they feel are not part of their group. This explains why some fans that support a football club might be hostile and biased when talking to people that do not support their club. This same pattern is seen in racial categorization. Some White-presenting people might be insensitive and harsh towards people from other races because they feel that they are not part of their race.

This is the reason some White-presenting people are comfortable with hurling racial abuses towards Visual

Minority people because they feel that they don't belong to their group. The solution to this problem is the extension of the group. What I mean by this is that instead of looking at people as Black, White, Native, or Asian, we can choose to look at people as human beings. When you look at people as human beings and remove the race label, you will see them as people that belong to the same group as you.

This perception will help you to avoid looking at people based on their race or culture but based on the fact that they are humans. This will help you to be more careful when talking to people that do not belong to your race. You will be less likely to discriminate against them or feel comfortable when others act towards them that way. So, we need to be more conscious about educating our people to stop labeling people based on their race but to see others as their brothers and sisters because we are all human beings.

Segregation

Some governmental policies show that there is discrimination against people from minority races in the US. For example, the system of "redlining" certain areas when deciding who can enjoy certain government policies is a reflection of how racism is embedded in the system subtly. What I mean by this is that there are mortgage policies where people that live in communities designated as "high risk" are not covered by government insurance. It is people from minority races that live in these neighborhoods. So, such policies are saying that people that belong to minority races are to be considered as "high risk," and cannot be trusted with government funds.

It is this subtle way of going about racism that has made it challenging for there to be concerted efforts to tackle it in our society. Many people will have been outraged if the policy says that Visual Minorities and other people belonging to minority races are not permitted to enjoy mortgage insurance. It would have been obvious that the government is showing favoritism towards some set of people. However, because it is not obvious, many White-presenting people would not agree with you when you tell them that they have privileges that are not available to Visual Minority people.

You will have to do more to convince others that racism is a problem today, unlike in the past. So, in a period where everyone is trying to sound politically correct, especially politicians, many things are said in a way that will not explicitly reflect racism. However, if you give them a second thought, you will realize that they have elements of segregation in them. If governmental policies show that certain people in society are not considered in the same way as others, why should citizens feel that people are the same? It is just natural that they would see Visual Minority people as second-class citizens.

However, racism will hardly be a conversation that is given the kind of urgency and attention it requires because it is not obvious. Historical racism is still embedded in the system, but it is hard to point it out in an era where racism is seen as socially unacceptable behavior. An average White-presenting American would agree that racism is wrong in front of a camera or when asked to fill out a survey. However, it is different in practice. The chances of getting your dream job or getting the opportunity you deserve as a Visual Minority are lower when a White-presenting person is tasked with judging the situation. You as a Visual Minority will have to do more than is expected of a White-presenting person before he or she would be convinced that you have what it takes.

Boundaries in real estate contribute to the limited interracial interaction in our communities that is increasing racial unfamiliarity. When Visual Minority people struggle to be able to purchase the kind of houses that a White-presenting person will find easier to buy, how are White-presenting people supposed to consider Visual Minority people as their equals? The gap needs to be closed so that there can be more Visual Minority people around the neighborhoods where there are White-presenting people to facilitate racial interaction, thereby reducing or even eliminating racism.

American Hierarchy

The reality is that some Americans are perceived to be more American than others. A White-presenting person might not know this or might deny it, but this is the reality of the situation. What I mean is that you hardly see any American that is White being referred to as "White American." However, you will see descriptions such as "Asian American" or "African American." When people talk about Americans, what usually comes to mind are the White-presenting people who are citizens of the nation. Most positive things are associated with being White. Even God or Jesus is depicted as White. This enhances the perception that White-presenting people are better leaders than Visual Minority people.

The disproportionately high number of White-presenting people that have higher social status and influence also contributes to racism in America. The fact that the number of White-presenting people that are in the elite bracket in society communicates the wrong idea that Visual Minority people are lazy and are suited for low life in the hood. We have had so many 'first Black Americans to do this' and 'first Black American to do that.' When a White American achieves a milestone, he or she is rarely referred to as 'the first White American' to achieve the feat.

For example, Barack Obama is often described as the first Black American to be the president of the US. In the same way, Kamala Harris is described as the first female, Black vice president of the US. The fact that we make a big deal out of the fact that a Visual Minority became the president or vice president shows how far we still have to go. Of course, it is a step in the right direction because it shows other Visual Minority people that it is possible to achieve considerable success if they are willing to give it their best and overcome the barriers in the system.

Still, it doesn't change the fact that the number of White-presenting people among the elite in society is disproportionately higher than Visual Minority people in this category. It is rare to find Visual Minority people among those at the helm of affairs in most top companies in the US. Even companies such as Wells Fargo that pride themselves on their vision to include people in the minority race among their decision-makers have not been able to deliver on their promises. The statement by the company's CEO that the reason it doesn't have Visual Minority people among its board members is due to a lack of talent led to a public outcry. After all is said and done, the American hierarchy is real.

Passivism

According to Roberts and Rizzo, passivism is the most insidious component of American racism. They concluded in a review of several studies that the disproportionate socioeconomic power that White-presenting Americans possess is already so great that they wouldn't even need to be active to maintain it. The key tools utilized by passivism through which racism prevails in America are ignorance of existing inequities and denial of historical racism. In other words, the fact that many people are ignorant of the fact that White-presenting people and Visual Minority people are not treated the same way in the nation makes them have no reason to protest against this anomaly. Unless you are a Visual Minority that has experienced this kind of treatment, you could be carried away too.

So, I am not too surprised that many White-presenting people are racially ignorant or racially neutral. If you want to understand the gravity of racism in our society, you will have to be deliberately observant to carry out your research. There is more than enough research-based evidence that shows that Visual Minority people and people of other minority races don't get the same treatment as White-presenting people in the US, Canada, or the UK. According to a study by Edwards and colleagues in 2019, about 1000 civilians are killed each year by law enforcement officers in the United States. Interestingly, Visual Minority men are 2.5 times more likely to be killed than White-presenting men by police in their lifetime, according to this study.

It is scary and alarming at the same time. Another study showed that Visual Minority people are twice as likely to be fatally shot by the police than White-presenting people, even when they are unarmed. According to Justin Nix, a criminologist at the University of Nebraska, Omaha, there is more than enough evidence that shows that action needs to be taken against this disproportionate killing of Visual Minority people by police. One thousand deaths a year is not normal. The fact that Visual Minority people are the most likely victims also speaks volumes. Sadly, new evidence has supported this racial bias in police killings.

A 2019 study revealed bias in administrative records is responsible for how some studies underestimate the levels of racial bias in policing. Some even try to mask discrimination entirely. A study showed that White-presenting officers dispatched to Visual Minority neighborhoods fired their guns five times more often than Visual Minority officers dispatched to the same places. Something is not right here. It is a sign that these White-presenting officers are products of racial bias and discrimination.

This might be the first time you have read about research-based evidence regarding the bias against Visual Minority people in the US. I will encourage you to do your study around this. What you will discover is that this same pattern of racial bias and discrimination is all over the sectors in the UK, Canada, and the US. So, you might not have experienced it as a Visual Minority or observed it as a White-presenting person. Still, the fact remains that the country is not the same for both Visual Minorities and White-presenting people. There is an America for White-presenting people and there is another one for Visual Minority people. Even though they live in the same country, the experience and treatment are not the same.

Chapter Nine:
Interracial Marriage & Relationships

Interracial relationships and marriages are a veritable yardstick for measuring the acceptance of Visual Minority people by White-presenting people. This is because it is not likely that you will be in a romantic relationship with a person unless you accept, love, and value the person. Besides, it also means that you accept his or her race and would see his or her family like yours. In this chapter, we will explore facts around interracial marriages and relationships in Canada and the US to continue our investigation on racial inequity.

Interracial Relationships and Marriage: Unfair FACTS

In the US, interracial marriage became legal in 1967, which made anti-miscegenation laws unconstitutional. Before then, interracial marriage was forbidden by the law in 31 states of the US. The judge concluded that the freedom to marry or not to marry a person of whatever race resides with the individual and cannot be infringed by the State. Since then, there has been an increase in interracial marriage. By 2010, 15.1% of all new marriages in the US were mixed race. Public approval of interracial marriage had also improved to 80% in the 2000s, unlike in the 1950s when it was 5%. This stat shows that things have improved in this regard, unlike in the mid-20th century.

However, a closer look shows that interracial marriage between White-presenting people and Visual Minorities is still low in comparison to other races. For example, according to a report by Pew Research, interracial marriage between White-presenting people and Hispanics was 42% of all interracial marriages between 2014 and 2015. In comparison, interracial marriage between White-presenting people and Visual Minorities was 11% during that period. So, although a lot had changed since 1960 when interracial marriage used to be illegal, there seems to remain a resentment regarding interracial marriage between White-presenting people and Visual Minorities in the US. Many White families are not willing to agree to have their children or relatives marry a person from a minority race, especially Visual Minorities.

In Canada, the story is similar. A 2011 study showed that couples composed of two Canadians by birth accounted for 66.9% of all married and common-law couples in that year. According to a poll by Ipsos for Global News, 15% of Canadians would never marry anyone that is outside their race. A 2011 National Household Survey also showed that only 4.6% of all married couples and common-law couples in Canada were mixed unions. Out of that number, 3.9% of all couples had one person who was not a visible minority and one that is a visible minority. Just like in the US, there is also resentment regarding getting into a relationship or married to someone that is not White-presenting.

Indeed, everyone has the right to choose who they want to marry. No one should be forced to marry whoever they don't want to marry. Usually, people get married because they feel that the other person has qualities that will add value to their lives. So, the fact that many White-presenting people are not willing to marry people from other races is a sign that they don't feel that they are people that can add value to their lives. Indeed, things are improving. Still, there is so much to do.

My Interracial Relationships

It's a lighter and funny story, and I like telling it. Before now, I have been trying to convince my White-presenting partner that White privilege exists, but at first, she didn't believe me. Everything I told her sounded vague to her. Just like my father, deep down, she had felt that I was only trying to give an excuse for some of my failures. There was no way I could let her see what I was trying to pass across to her. Over time, I got tired of trying to convince her because it was always a futile effort. Besides, the arguments around racism were beginning to get heated between us.

So, for the sake of not doing something that would affect our relationship, I stopped talking to her about it. I knew that she would eventually understand me someday when she experiences it. Before now, most of the times that I have been treated differently or harshly due to my skin color, she had not witnessed them. I wished she would be there someday to understand what I was talking about. Therefore, when we had this experience, I was a little happy because she finally got to see what I have been trying to communicate all this while. We were together in 2013 when this incident occurred right before her eyes. My partner and I were on our way to visit her mother in Florida from Toronto, and we decided to try and save money by taking a connecting flight to Atlanta Airport.

Now, before we go any further, I have to tell you that all my life, I've felt watched by airport security due to racial profiling. For me, I have to alter my appearance to lower the probability of being profiled. My White-presenting partner at the time was blind to the invisibility of inequality, and so I didn't discuss it with her because I felt she wasn't ready to see the world through my eyes.

She used to wonder why I didn't know the airport security protocols as well as she did and why I seemed easily 'confused' during check-ins and waiting in line. Later, she learned it was because I avoided traveling to evade feeling the battle fatigue guarding against profiling (which is caused by the way I look as an Unidentifiable Visual Minority), which tends to attract more scrutiny from airport security in various parts of the world.

This means I have to make sure I'm clean-shaven and take my hat off, avoid wearing black, and remember to smile a lot and avoid any serious conversation. I've found this helps security see me as less of a possible threat. But I've secretly been envious of White-presenting people at the airport. They get to dress how they want, wear what they want, say what they want at any volume, and get to avoid the kind of attention from security I'm used to adapting to. This would be an experience that would help make the invisibility of inequality a little more visible to my White-presenting partner. Before this incident, I had never been to Atlanta International, and when we got there, I was astonished.

I had never seen so many Visual Minority people before at an airport with relevant careers. Diversity was everywhere. Except for White-presenting pilots, as far as I could tell, Visual Minority people ran the airport operations almost entirely. I felt myself smile as I realized I was feeling a little more like I fit in. At other airports, I've always been on-guard and spring-loaded to react with stressed civility.

No doubt you've guessed the crux of this story happened at Atlanta security. We were waiting in line as usual. In my mind, I was multitasking by anticipating and rehearsing short answers to security questions (the standard practice of mine). We got to the front of the line, and I realized I had a hat on (to me, this was a cardinal rule now broken).

I looked at the Visual Minority customs officer and said, 'Sorry sir,' as I scrambled to take my hat off. To my surprise, he said, 'Don't worry about it,' and gave me a calming look. I still put my hat away in my pocket, but I felt a gentle wave of relaxation wash over me. It was like my request to relax was officially heard. Then it happened. I walked past the male Visual Minority customs officer and met a female White-presenting customs officer who noticed I had put 'something' in my pocket and stopped me. She said somewhat sternly, 'Sir I need to see what you just put in your pocket.' Again, to my surprise, the Visual Minority customs officer behind me yelled, 'Nah, Stacey, I already approved, let him go.' She looked a little annoyed as she stepped back and let me pass.

I felt entitled, empowered, and a little bit privileged for the first time in an airport. I looked over to my right and noticed another Visual Minority customs officer. No doubt he had witnessed my interaction with Stacey, the customs officer. He looked my way and gave me a very subtle, reassuring nod. It was as though he and I had had an entire conversation over that situation, in that nod. I felt understood, and I felt safe. I thought, is this how White-presenting people feel all the time around security?

I felt acquitted from all flavors of prejudice and so much confidence that I said to the nodding customs officer, 'Do I know you, sir?' Did we go to high school or something? His professional expression leaked into laughter as I stood up a little straighter and happily walked (almost swaggered) past Stacey, the White-presenting customs officer. A moment later, I looked over my shoulder and noticed my partner was still behind me. She had been randomly stopped by airport security (also a Visual Minority like me). I calmly watched from a distance as they asked her to step aside and agree to be scanned from head to toe. A couple of minutes passed. When it was over, she looked a little annoyed, and a bit confused, turned to me, and said, 'That's never happened to me before, why did that take so long? And why didn't they stop anyone else?'

Immediately, I felt a strong opportunity to try and relate and to explain to her the kernel of a very complicated topic that I knew she had no direct reference to or experience with. However, to me, we had now shared an experience that I thought helped a little to put us on equal footing. Meaning, at this moment, her White-entitlement advantages were suddenly gone, and I wanted to take this opportunity to help her sort out an understanding of why this moment was inexplicably uncomfortable. But I knew she wasn't ready to have such an uncomfortable and deep conversation over something so small. So, instead, I casually said to her, 'Now you know what it's like to be a Visual Minority.' She flashed a very confused look and quickly forgot about the experience, but to me, this was the beginning of my White-presenting partner's deep understanding of the invisibility of inequality. However, it would take years and another trip to the airport for her to truly feel what words could not articulate.

As far as I am concerned, interracial relationships should be the norm rather than an exception. It should not be shocking that people who are not from the same race decided to get into a romantic relationship that ended up in marriage. Race should not be the determinant of a successful marriage but the individual qualities of the couple. I am glad that my partner understands that, and it has been able to help us to build a robust relationship that is founded on mutual respect for one another. Just like any relationship, we have had our issues, and we are still a work in progress. It is not perfect, but we are willing to make compromises to overlook the things that are secondary to focus on the essential things.

The trend I have observed from reports, polls, and studies is that it seems Americans and Canadians that are younger are more open to marrying someone that is not from their race than the older generations. This shows that it is likely that things change over time, and we will record more interracial marriages. However, the influence of the older generations is still strong on the younger generation. So, it might take time before it becomes the norm that a White-presenting person gets married to a Visual Minority in the US and Canada.

My Visual Minority Mother and Her Family

My Visual Minority mother and her family have certain values that my White father and his family do not share. My Visual Minority mother and her family are kind people who love their own and values mutual respect. The same can be said about my White-presenting father and his family. However, unlike my White-presenting father and his family, my Visual Minority mother and her family are more direct.

They don't say what they don't mean. If they don't like you, they would never pretend that they do. If you do something they don't like, they will tell you straight to your face without caring what you think. I learned to be straightforward and deal with issues squarely from them. I admire their honesty because they are not likely to act in your absence the other way round from the way they do in your presence. Their approach to things leads to arguments sometimes, especially when dealing with defensive people. However, they prefer to let people know what they think about them rather than gossip when they are not around.

If they say anything about someone while the person was not there, you can be sure that they would still tell the person to his or her face later. They are passionate people who would defend their own with all that they have. They are courageous people who are never afraid to air their opinion. It never matters to them even when the other person doesn't accept or respect what they have to say.

As earlier mentioned, they are not as educated as my White-presenting father and his family. Also, they don't enjoy the same privileges that are enjoyed by their White-presenting counterparts. Still, they have many things money cannot buy. They are resilient people who wouldn't let anything bring them down. They are products of many battles that they have won against the tides of life. They are tough on the outside, but they have big hearts.

They are not against people from their race getting married to people from other races. However, they would not take it lightly with anyone who doesn't show respect to their relatives or their family. They respect my father and his family, but they are never afraid to air their opinion whenever they feel that certain things should not be done in a certain way.

My White Father and His Family

An obvious difference between my Visual Minority mother and her family and my White-presenting father and his family is in their approach to things. The fact that they are more educated contributed to their advantage. Of course, they are not racially ignorant. However, in my mind, many are racially neutral. They have never had to impose themselves before they are respected or taken seriously, unlike my mother and her family.

So, it is easy for them to dismiss any discussion regarding racism. They are aware that interracial marriage between families is set on an edge. As a result of this, they always do anything necessary to protect the integrity of the relationship. I commend them for this. Unlike my mother and her family, my father and his family are always keen to avoid certain controversies. They are reserved people who are always seeking ways to end a potentially disrupting situation as soon as possible. As a whole, they taught me to be a gentleman who should earn respect rather than demand it.

It is easier for them to say that because they present as White-presenting people who don't have to strive for recognition like Visual Minorities. An example of this was when I was younger and was a victim of a bully called Roger (a story I told earlier). That incident made the chasm between the way White-presenting people and Visual Minority people are treated obviously to me. Of course, sometimes I also wonder whether my father was more respected than my mother because he is a man, and my mother is a woman. However, after watching how White-presenting women are treated sometimes, I realize that the gulf in difference has more to do with racial inequity rather than gender inequality.

This particular incident between Roger and me happened a long time ago, but I have not forgotten and will never forget it because of its multifaceted lessons and realities. It was an experience that consolidated what I have always suspected about the difference between whether Visual Minority people and White-presenting people are taken seriously or not. It was a moment that laid it all bare for me as to why many Visual Minority people have to assert themselves to be heard while in comparison, it is sometimes effortless for many White-presenting people to do the same.

Societal Norms and Perceptions

In the US and Canada, the perception of interracial marriage is improving compared to what it used to be. It increased by 15.1% in 2010 and reached an all-time high of 8.4% in the same year. Still, many people are skeptical about the success of such marriages. Recent trends show that interracial marriages often happen between people that share similar characteristics, such as income, education, and age. For example, in about one-in-five of each group, the couples are college graduates. So, it appears that the husbands and wives that were able to look beyond the race of their partners were more interested in other qualities they felt were more valuable than skin color.

It was noticed in a study by Pew Research, that the combined annual earnings of interracial couples in 2010 were $56,700. Also, the average age of brides was 32, and the age gap was similar between husband and wife. Interestingly, when it comes to the combined annual earnings of interracial couples, the low earnings of Visual Minority people show up. For example, in 2010, the combined annual earnings of White/Asian couples was $71,000 while it was $58,000 for White/Hispanic couples. White/Black couples were the lowest with $53,000. Sadly, this same trend was noticed when the educational levels of interracial couples were considered. In this category, White/Asian couples were the most educated, with the couples likely to be college graduates.

About six in ten Asian newlyweds that married White-presenting people were college graduates. This figure was far less when it came to the situation where a Visual Minority married a White-presenting individual. A lot needs to change in this regard. Still, there are reasons for optimism. For example, it was observed in a study by Pew Research, that as the number of interracial marriages has increased in the US and Canada, public opinion is also changing. For example, four-in-ten Americans (43%) believe that interracial marriages will change our society. These people believe that the change will be positive. However, 10% believe that interracial marriage will change our society for the worse.

There are reasons to be skeptical about this result because most of the people that believe that interracial relationships and marriages will improve society are minorities, more educated, liberals, and those living in the Western or Eastern states in the US. The study also showed that 35% of American adults say that they have a close relative that married someone from a different race. Also, 63% said that they wouldn't have issues with a relative getting married to someone from a different race. In comparison to the past, things are getting better in this regard. Still, there is a lot of ground to be covered because the number of people that are against interracial marriages in the US and Canada is still unacceptably high.

Chapter Ten:
Modern-Day Racism

If modern racism was still as obvious as it used to be in the slave trade era, it would have been easier to tackle it. The fact that it is under the radar makes it easy for people to perpetuate it without raising eyebrows. Only the victims know that racial segregation is still in full force despite the abolishment of Jim Crowe laws. In this chapter, we will explore the invisible nature of modern-day racism.

Difficulty With Explaining Racism To Racially Ignorant People

One of the dilemmas I have always had is how I could explain what racism feels like to racially ignorant people. It is not because I lack the words to use or the ability to explain my thoughts, rather the issue is that I don't know how to communicate it in such a way that a person will be able to understand how people are subjected to racial discrimination feel. How is a person, that has not and will never have any reason to be subjected to racial discrimination, to understand how such people feel?

So, the issue has never been how to explain or conjure the words to use. Instead, it has always been how to make racially ignorant people understand how it feels when someone else is a victim. The only hope is comparing it with religious segregation. Still, it does not portray the real picture of racism. As earlier mentioned, religion is a choice people make. You can choose to change your religious affiliation for whatever reasons or as a result of a change in conviction. There have been people who used to be Muslims that became Christians, and vice versa. There have also been people who used to be Christians that claimed they are now agnostics or atheists.

However, you cannot change your race. Even if you bleach your skin and undergo various cosmetic surgeries, it still doesn't change who you are. So, using religious segregation to help explain racial discrimination to a racially ignorant person cannot be sufficient. In many ways, experience is the best teacher. When something has never happened to you, you might not be able to understand how others feel when they experience it. For example, if you have never experienced a divorce, you might never understand the challenges of moving on and starting a new life. When you advise a person experiencing a divorce, you might be quick to tell the person to move on and forget the past.

The best option indeed is for the person to move on and face the future with optimism. However, you will be doing the person a disservice when you don't acknowledge the pain that the person has as a result of the situation. Sadly, pain cannot be communicated; it can only be experienced. There is no amount of explanation that can paint a better picture about pain than the experience of it. So, it is incredibly challenging to explain the pain of a person, that is subjected to racial discrimination, to a racially ignorant person. Some people might stop for a while, especially when they care about the person that is hurt by their actions.

Yet, they might start acting that way again towards someone else because they are yet to understand what others feel when they experience racial discrimination. The issue with racial slurs and actions is that they often trigger several other problems for the person. Insulting people by using racially insensitive words can make them begin to question the reason for their existence, especially if they are facing certain challenges in other aspects of their lives. So, an apology cannot always undo the damage of racially insensitive actions and words, and this is what is difficult to explain to racially ignorant folks.

If you are racially ignorant, and the person has a forgiving heart, he or she might forgive you if you offend them. Still, if you have unintentionally offended him or her, that offense will keep burning and hurting the person long after the words have been uttered. The power of words is a phenomenon that many authors have explored. Offensive words have a way of staying in our hearts for years, even when we have forgiven the person that said them to us. For example, a parent might call a child a simpleton in annoyance and apologize to the child later. The child might forgive the parent, but it may take a long time before the child will be able to fight off the effects of what was said to him or her. So, apologizing for racial abuse is not enough to heal the victim. It should not be happening in the first place.

The Subtlety of Modern Racism

The subtlety of racism compounds like monetary interest over time. Many or all racist White-presenting people deny their affiliation with racism to maintain optics that keep their entitlement intact. On the other hand, some Visual Minority people are so sensitive to racism that they can feel the presence of a racist situation when White-presenting people are unaware of it because White privilege is intended to block White-presenting people from learning about racist oppression. This is the reason I believe that my father didn't engage with me in any conversation about racism. He has a Visual Minority son from a mixed marriage and never had a reason to be a victim of the oppression that comes through racism.

So, it is understandable that he seemed to give me the impression that racism is just a façade. He may have seen the world through his lenses of being married to a Visual Minority woman. However, many White-presenting people are not like that. Yet, it hurts to feel he didn't want to have that conversation with me. I have seen this same unwillingness to discuss issues of racism peacefully with many White-presenting people. Many of them cannot even see the link between historical racism and what we have at the moment. Many of them believe that racists today are just foolish people who love to treat people wrongly.

Indeed, there will always be people in this world that disrespect people for various reasons, including gender, religion, and social class. Yet, you cannot deny that the reason some White-presenting people see Visual Minority people as individuals that belong to an inferior race is linked to the slave era. Many of them still feel entitled because their ancestors were slave owners, while the ancestors of Visual Minority people were the slaves who had no freedom and spent most or at least part of their lives in bondage to please their White-presenting masters.

Political Correctness Or Deafening Silence

Political correctness refers to speaking, especially publicly. in such a way that the beliefs and values of others are respected. It was meant to help curb insensitive statements and jokes about racism, sexuality, and religion. Instead, it is fast becoming the tool that is leading to a deafening silence on sensitive issues. In the name of being politically correct, many people are unwilling to speak about racism because they don't want to say something that might sound offensive. This has made it easy for politicians and individuals that are racist to keep their opinions away from the media.

Even when they are racists, people wouldn't admit it in our world today. They know that the world is watching and any action or words that are racially insensitive would be frowned at unlike back in the days when they could speak freely. Many people rightly condemn the actions of former American President, Donald Trump for his racially insensitive words. While he was in office, the unemployment rate of African Americans was 5.5%, which is the worst since the US Department of Labor started collecting data in the 1970s. He often claims that he is not racist, obviously to sound politically correct but his actions often say otherwise.

During his campaign for the American presidency, he made explicit racist remarks, such as referring to Mexican immigrants as criminals and rapists. He also once stereotyped a Visual Minority reporter and was on the side of white supremacists that held a violent rally to mock the Trail of Tears. Trump's case is a perfect depiction of the nature of racism in the modern world. People deny it but it is never far away. It keeps staring us in the face while many people are not aware of its existence.

Even when some White-presenting people agree that racism exists and believe that it is a problem, they don't see it as anything that poses a grave threat in such a way that it has to be dealt with as soon as possible. This is one of the reasons it has always been difficult to generate the kind of pull or energy that is needed to stamp out systemic and deliberate racism from our society.

White-presenting People Downplaying Racist Stories

The body language of many White-presenting people when Visual Minority people talk about racism, suggests that this problem might not be solved any time soon. Like my White-presenting father, and my White-presenting partner once did, many White-presenting people downplay Visual Minority racist stories to soften how it affects Visual Minorities in a misguided attempt to protect them from modern racism. But it is interpreted by Visual Minority people as insulting because it may suggest Visual Minority people are just looking for attention or being dramatic, and therefore not to be taken seriously. You really cannot blame those downplaying White-presenting people because they rarely hear these stories of Visual Minority inequity live and on a one-to-one basis.

Even Donald Trump claims that he is not a racist. Racist White-presenting people know that they would be verbally attacked if they come out plainly to admit that they are racists. So, whenever they are asked publicly in an interview, they would claim that they see all people as equal even when that is not what they believe. Visual Minority people encounter racism by the day in the UK, US, and Canada. Yet, many White-presenting people downplay this reality unless you show them facts, or they witness incidents as devastating as the George Floyd or Emit Till's case.

For example, they would say, "Come on, it's not that bad." This was perfectly portrayed by a Colombian I met that immigrated to Canada. He said that his perception of a lot of White-presenting girls he met in Canada was that they don't believe how the racial problems he has endured are very serious and more violent compared to similar problems in Canada. He said a common phrase he heard when sharing his stories of inequity was "Come on, it's not that bad." This upset him because the response sounded dismissive, even if the intention may have been that they were trying to make him calm down.

We don't have to wait until Visual Minority people are lynched on live TV by White supremacists before we know that we need to do something about this issue. Dismissing it as something that is not that serious, when Visual Minority people complain about the problem, will only make more people suffer in silence, which is not an ideal situation for any human being.

The Invisible Enemy

Modern racism has been able to camouflage itself in various ways, and political correctness is one of them. We cannot proceed to evolve if we are not willing to have conversations about racism. If there is a problem in our family, it will never go away if we keep treating it like a taboo topic. Yes, racism can indeed generate a lot of negative emotions and discomfort. Yet, we must be willing to have open, honest, peaceful, and respectful, conversations about it.

Until we are willing to do so, racism will continue to be that invisible enemy that is affecting us all, with Visual Minority people as the victims of this menace, and White-presenting people having the option to simply ignore or forget about it. We have to be our brothers' and sisters' keepers. You might not be directly affected by racism as a White Visual Minority person. Still, that does not mean that you should ignore it or dismiss it when Visual Minority people complain about it.

Chapter Eleven:
Fact-Checking And Statistics Studies In North America In The Last 200 Years Or More

We will move a notch higher on this journey by exploring facts that support the presence of racial inequity in the US and Canada. We are moving in this direction because our arguments must be based on facts and not just emotions. I have shared many of my personal experiences with you, so far, to show you why I believe that there is racial inequity in these two nations. However, many people often feel that I am just sentimental. So, at this point, let's explore what studies have discovered regarding this sensitive topic in the US and Canada.

The Invention Of Firearms Leading To Enforced Slavery

The wide use of fireworks in North America could have made many North Americans believe that fireworks are North American inventions. However, this is not true. Fireworks were invented in China thousands of years ago. It was an accidental innovation that occurred when a Chinese chemist mixed saltpeter (potassium nitrate) with sulfur and charcoal, which created gunpowder. The charcoal caught the flame that initiated the chemical process, while the saltpeter created the force that blasted out to make the cracking and popping sound. The sulfur was responsible for the showering visual display. Afterward, the Chinese started using fireworks during various festivals.

Europeans began to use saltpeter to develop gunpowder, and the invention of firearms made gunpowder vital when weaponized. Records from history showed that three King's gunpowder makers were working in the Tower of London in 1515. The English Civil war between 1642 and 1645, led to an expansion of this industry because it was largely used during this period. In the 14th century, European manufacturers improved the combustion and consistency of gunpowder through a process called **corning**, which involves the drying of gunpowder into small clumps. This advancement in weaponry gave Europeans the edge to colonize African nations.

However, the Europeans were not involved in slave trading on the West African coast before the 16th century. The Portuguese were the first European nation to use African slaves. They were used in gold mines and on sugar plantations on the small equatorial island of Sao Tome. These plantations became the model that was used in subsequent sugar plantations in the West Indies. During these periods, African Exports included palm oil, gold, cloth, gum, ivory, pepper, yams, and nuts. The first foundations of globalization were laid in the first century when African rulers forged trading relationships with

European traders. Initially, the English were not interested in taking slaves, but things changed soon afterward.

The intense rivalry for West Africa began to heat up among Europeans. However, they were more interested in obtaining human cargo along the West African coast than conquering the interior. During the 1590s, the Portuguese monopoly of slave trading was challenged by the Dutch. Later, nations like Sweden, Denmark, and Scotland became interested. In 1667, the British captured the forts built by the Portuguese and Dutch on the Gold Coast (Ghana). West African rulers were instrumental in facilitating the slave trade by exchanging their prisoners of war for firearms. The kings and chiefs were using their newly acquired firearms to expand their territory, which led to an increase in tension and violence.

As a result of the invention and use of firearms, Britain, Spain, France, and Portugal were able to enforce slavery in various parts of the world, which contributed to the devaluation of the equality of people. So, once some people were seen as slaves, especially Africans, things didn't change, even long after the slave trade era was over. In the US during the 17th century, legally sanctioned racism made Native Americans, African Americans, Latino Americans, and Americans from lesser developed parts of Europe incapable of enjoying rights granted to European Americans. For example, European Americans were privileged by law in matters of literacy, voting rights, immigration, citizenship, criminal procedure, and land acquisition.

Also, numerous European ethnic groups, including Irish and Jews, were subjected to xenophobic exclusion and other forms of racism in American society during this period. Racially structured institutions, such as Native American reservations, Indian Wars, residential schools (for Native Americans), and internment camps (for Japanese Americans) showed the segregation that continued to exist. Formal racial discrimination was largely banned in the mid-20th century. However, historic racism continued to reflect in the modern US and Canadian society in the form of racial stratification in employment, education, housing, government, and lending. Many people in the US, Canada, and Europe still show some form of prejudice towards other races, even today. The era of the slave masters and colonial masters is gone. However, the impact of their dehumanizing activities and inequity still pervades the US and Canadian society.

Racial Bias In The US And Canada In The Last 200 Years

The truth is, that we all have preferences and sentiments in every situation. As a football fan, you might choose to support one athlete or the other. In your fashion sense, you might prefer items that have a touch of red instead of the ones that have a touch of purple. You also have the right to choose your friends. You might prefer to hang out with rich people to enhance your career as an entrepreneur. When it comes to dating, you might prefer chubby people to slim individuals. It is never a problem. However, it is a serious issue when you disrespect people and treat them like nonentities because they don't like the things you like or are not part of the kind of people you like to roll with.

Using this same logic, for whatever reason, you might prefer to hang out with White-presenting people or Visual Minority people. This is not an issue. You might prefer to hang out with White-presenting friends, but if you are an employer, you should never consider a person's race when making professional decisions regarding job opportunities. This is exactly the problem we are facing in the US and Canada, even today. People allow their racial bias to affect the way they treat people and the way they give them the opportunities to achieve success in life. The facts behind this reality are brutal. For example, when you consider disparities between average family wealth by Caucasian and Visual Minority people in the USA and Canada in the last 200 years, you will discover that something isn't right somewhere.

According to a report by the New York Times in September 2020, the US has the highest wealth gap in the world although it is the richest nation in the world! The report revealed that per capita wealth grew more than 13% in 2019 in the US. This study implies that the super-rich in the US is getting richer and leaving the rest behind. The pandemic only came to exacerbate the situation. Of course, this fact is disturbing enough. Still, it gets worse when you realize the kind of people that are in the super-rich category and the ones that are below the economic food chain.

In 2014, according to Statista, close to 25% of families within the less than ten thousand dollars income bracket, were Visual Minorities. It gets worse when you investigate the ethnicity of the millionaires in the US. As of 2013, 76% of the millionaires in the US are White-presenting people. Asian Americans and Visual Minority Americans account for 8% of this population. The gulf separation is appalling. The chances that this number changes anytime soon is slim when you consider the fact that Visual Minority Americans represent a huge number of unemployed Americans. As of 2020, 11.4% of Visual Minority Americans are unemployed, which is only worse than Puerto Ricans (11.7%).

White-presenting people have the least number of unemployed people, with 7.3%. Remember that White-presenting people are the majority ethnic group. The fact that a minority ethnic group has a higher unemployment rate than the major ethnic group in a nation should make us wonder what exactly is happening. This statistic implies that while White-presenting people are likely to get richer because they are employed, Visual Minorities do not have the same opportunity to strive for success due to unemployment. How can you dream of becoming a millionaire when you don't even have a job in the first place?

Affirmative Action

Affirmative action refers to a policy that intends to increase job or educational opportunities for underrepresented people. In the context of ethnicity, it refers to actions taken to deliberately include people of minority races in employment and education plans. Interestingly, it is banned in nine states in the US. Companies often claim that they plan to give job opportunities to people of minority races, but research says something else. According to a study published in 2004, resumes with "White-sounding" names have a higher chance of getting callbacks for interviews than the ones with "Black-sounding" names. This reality is making many Visual Minority people consider adding a White-sounding nickname to their resume to boost their chances of being given an opportunity.

Why is being a Visual Minority connected to mediocrity and lack of efficiency? According to Harvard Business School, minorities who "Whiten" job resumes get more interviews. According to the study, African American and Asian job applicants who mask their race on resumes have higher chances of getting job interviews. They go about this by deleting references to their race with the expectation that it will boost their chances. Sadly, it is paying off. It is a terrible sign that discriminatory practices exist even in organizations that claim to value diversity. According to the James M. Collins Visiting Associate Professor of Business Administration at Harvard Business School, Katherine A. DeCelles, discrimination still exists in the workplace and companies need to recognize this issue as soon as possible and address it.

It is unacceptable that anyone should be worried about their ethnicity when applying for a job. Rather, what anyone should be worried about should be their competence and attitude. However, it is a sad reality that many people belonging to minority races are tempted to make tweaks here and there to make their resumes "White enough" to get the opportunity they ought to earn strictly based on their ability to add value. These findings imply that White kids are given the platform to keep building and amassing while other races have to scramble for crumbs. The fact that the wealth gap between White-presenting people and other races is wide is never the issue. What hurts is that the path to close that gap is blocked.

Like NF said in a song, "How are you supposed to get a break when the doors ain't opened?" Understandably, there are more White-presenting millionaires in the US than any other race based on the history of racial inequity that has given White-presenting people an undue advantage from the start. However, what is frustrating is that we claim that the era of racism and slave trade is gone but many of its elements are still much too active today. Despite several politicians bringing up the issue in their bid to resolve it, none has ever been able to proffer a tangible solution to this problem.

Annoyingly, sometimes, when a Visual Minority brings up this issue, many White-presenting people, including my father and other people I have cited in this book, either intimate it does not exist or claim it does not exist. They think you are just trying to give an excuse for your failure or your laziness. Yet, the facts stare us in the face. Segregation and racial discrimination have ensured that we have a society where White-presenting people will continue to thrive and have less to worry about while people belonging to other races will have to keep working harder to have a chance against the odds that are stacked against them.

Skin Mis-Matching

Why are most Barbie dolls and band-aids more likely to match White-presenting people's skin the most? Have you ever thought about this question? The reality is that racism is still very much around, but it has become more challenging to identify it, especially if you are racially ignorant or racially neutral. The subtle impact of racism is seen even in Barbie dolls. The truth is that Barbie is more than a doll. It has become a global icon that carries a lot of symbolism with it. Otherwise, it would not have courted the controversies that have surrounded it over the years. Women rights activists protested against it in 2013 during the unveiling of Europe's first life-sized 'Barbie Dreamhouse,' claiming it is sexist.

They felt it placed unnecessary pressure on ladies to try to look beautiful, making them waste their potential and stagnating them in other areas of life. If Barbie dolls can be sexist, can they be racist too? Historically, Barbie dolls are White, busty, and thin. However, in the bid to make them more inclusive, the manufacturers have introduced various skin tones, body sizes, hair textures, and ability statuses. These changes were meant to encourage children of all races to be able to find a Barbie they can play with that looks like them. The first "Black Barbie" was released in 1980, long after the Civil Rights Movements and Chicano Movement. The question is, why did it have to take that long before they were produced?

Why did the manufacturers wait until they were pressured by the public before they realized that by creating only White dolls, they were promoting racial inequality? Are we to believe that a White-favored mindset has left the company simply because it bowed to public pressure to create Barbie dolls for minority races? This has made the intent of the company questionable in my mind. Are they creating Barbie dolls for minority races because they feel they should be treated as equal to White-presenting people or because it was going to affect their sales and public image? We will never know the real answer to this question.

Besides, White Barbie dolls match perfectly with the skin tone of Caucasian people but the same cannot be said about others. Could this be a result of the company lacking the skills and ability to create such products or a lack of commitment due to an inherent disregard and disrespect for minority races? In their defense, it could be argued that they have been making White Barbie dolls for years, which has helped them to perfect the art of creating them. However, there could also be a psychological basis for it. It could be because the manufacturers believe that White-presenting people would criticize them if they don't get their skin tone perfectly, which could have devastating impacts on their sales.

On the other hand, even if they don't get the skin tones of minority races perfectly, their complaints and criticism wouldn't mean much. I am not saying that I am very sure that this is the reason for the actions of the company. I am simply giving you various perspectives to analyze the situation. We have a responsibility to identify any form of racial inequality and address them in our society. We need to let every individual, institution, and organization, that are found in perpetuating racism either overtly or covertly, know that it is not acceptable.

Ethnicity In Digital Job Applications

If you have applied for digital jobs, you might have noticed that there are columns demanding ethnicity. For years, I kept wondering why this was necessary. A weak defense of this practice is that it is necessary to help the institution include people of minority races in their organization to promote diversity. It doesn't make sense in any way. We are advocating that Visual Minorities and people from other minority races should be allowed to show what they can do without considering the color of their skin. This does not mean that we are demanding that Visual Minority people should be given opportunities at the expense of White-presenting people.

All we are demanding is a level playing field for all, regardless of whether you are White or a Visual Minority. It is this lack of understanding that made some people start shouting "White Lives Matters" or "All Lives Matters" during the Black Lives Matter movement. The reality is that no one has to demand the rights of White-presenting people because everything is already designed to their advantage. What is urgent is for the rights of people of minority races to be respected. They should be tested and subjected to whatever is expected of any potential employee. If any company is serious about diversity, it does not need to include ethnicity in its job application. Requiring the race of an applicant puts them under unnecessary stress in a White-dominant society.

The National Bureau of Economic Research pointed out the fact that job applicants with White names usually send up to ten resumes to get a callback. On the other hand, it will take up to fifteen resumes for those with African Americans to get one callback. Companies keep claiming that they are working towards diversity and trying to eliminate segregation. There are even legislations that make it punishable when anyone is subjected to racial discrimination. However, how can you punish anyone that didn't tell you that he is denying you the opportunity you deserve because of your race? You cannot report such a case to the police because you know that you will have nothing tangible to prove to them.

Findings from various studies over the years have confirmed our fears. Job applicants from minority races have three options today. They can either choose to tick their real race, lie that they are White, or ignore the question altogether if it is not mandatory. The reality is that we all want to be given the chance to work hard to achieve our dreams in life. Psychologists explain that frustration is a product of the inability to achieve a goal. At this rate, many Visual Minority people will get more frustrated by the day because the color of their skin has become the only error they have committed. It is the reason they are profiled by security officers and it is also the reason they may be denied job opportunities.

Another cause for concern is the fact that ethnicity questions usually begin with 'Caucasian' and end with 'Other.' Why should it start that way? Is it just a coincidence? The fact that 'Caucasian' is mentioned first all the time, shows the race that is held in the highest esteem. For a change, companies should stop asking potential employees about their race. They should be able to look at the resumes of job applicants and decide who should be given the opportunity based on their qualifications and skills. It is not just a cliché. Research has shown that it affects the employment opportunities of people.

Racial Battle Fatigue For Visual Minority People

In 2008, Critical Race Theorist William Smith coined the term **Racial Battle Fatigue** (RBF). Initially, it was a term that was used to describe the experiences of African Americans in America, but it has now been extended to all People of Color in the US. It refers to the cumulative result of race-related stress response to distressing emotional and mental conditions. It leads to various forms of emotional, mental, and physical strain, which can cause psychological symptoms. Some of the symptoms of RBF include increased sickness, suppressed immunity, tension headaches, chronic pain, elevated blood pressure, a pounding heartbeat, and trembling.

Also, when People of Color with RBF expect themselves to be exposed to racially motivated conflicts, it can lead to an upset stomach, rapid breathing, or frequent urination. Anxiety, increased swearing, ulcers, insomnia, emotional withdrawal, rapid mood swings, and difficulty in speaking coherently, are also symptoms of RBF. All of these can make People of Color lose their self-confidence and self-worth. It could also affect their self-efficacy. In other words, it could affect the way a person believes he or she can succeed in a task before attempting it. People develop RBF after experiencing racism for a prolonged period, in a predominantly White space.

It can lead to poor health attitudes, such as lack of exercise and poor eating habits, which can make the immune system weaker and make a person susceptible to diseases. Complications from RBF, such as hypertension, can end up leading to the death of a person. White-presenting people have no idea what it means to experience this kind of situation and will never experience it. That is why many of them don't understand the pain and anguish racism can cause. Many think that racist abuses are supposed to be regular abuses people should ignore. It is the sign of ignorance about the pain of this experience that makes people talk that way.

How can you ignore racial slurs when you are also finding it difficult to get good grades or job opportunities because of your skin color? Racism has all manner of implications, including health and finance. It batters the self-esteem of the victims. It makes them feel like they are not human beings. These are not the kind of feelings any human being should have. Even criminals should not be dehumanized. Sadly, we live in a society where animal rights matter more than the rights of minority races. Things could be different if Visual Minorities get the kind of sympathy that animals get when they are maltreated by people.

Visual Minorities try to make ends meet in a predominantly White environment while fighting to keep their physical and mental health at the same time. To say that this is not fair is an understatement. It is too much to ask from a human being. Life is tough already. As a Visual Minority, it is double trouble. You have to face the regular adversity that comes to you in life, then you also have to face the unpleasant circumstances you find yourself in because of the color of your skin.

Chapter Twelve:
Racial Inequity Specific To Canada And The Us

This chapter is a continuation of the line of thought we started exploring in the last section. We will explore more facts and evidence that support the existence of racial inequity in Canada and the US. However, we will be more detailed here and will discuss the two nations separately.

Racial Inequity In Canada

The following incidents and disappointing situations reflect the source, depth, and reasons racism might not go away anytime soon in Canada:

Visual Minority Slaves Ownership By Early Canadians

It might sound disturbing and worrisome, but the reality is that the enslavement of African people was legal in Canada before 1834. It was a veritable means of sustaining colonial economic enterprise. Via its history of international trade, Canada was involved in the transatlantic slave trade before it was eventually abolished. During this period, slave-produced goods such as molasses, rum, sugar, and tobacco were exchanged for salted cod and timber. The people involved in this dehumanizing activity saw it as a cheap means of labor in comparison to having to pay European workers. This is perhaps the reason some employees still struggle to want to pay White and Visual Minority people the same amount of money even today.

The slaves were nothing more than the property that could be bought and sold at will. Even after the British were defeated in the American Revolution, it didn't reduce the number of enslaved Africans. Instead, it increased because the Canadian government passed the Imperial Statute of 1790, which allowed United Empire Loyalists to bring their household furniture, clothing, utensils of husbandry, and Negros, duty-free. As you would have noticed, they mentioned African slaves in the same breath as other properties. It was indeed a humiliation. It was so bad that advertisements for the sale of slaves appeared in newspapers.

To cap it all, slave-owning was a practice that people from all levels of early Canadian society had. This included government officials, military officials, hotel keepers, and fur traders. Sadly, even priests, bishops, and nuns had slaves. For example, the priest of Saint-Antoine-sur-Richelieu, Father Louis Payet, owned five slaves. Four of them were Black, while one was indigenous. Also, it is noteworthy that six out of the sixteen members of the first parliament of the Upper Canada Legislative Assembly owned slaves.

Reparations For Canadian Slave Owners

Reparation refers to compensation due to people who were victims of injustice during a particular period. For all the years of abuse, misuse, and violent acts against Visual Minority slaves, it is expected that a form of apology or compensation would be given to the descendants of these people. However, it has proven to be problematic due to many reasons. We are talking about people who were treated like animals and tortured to death in some cases. A classic example was the case of a Visual Minority slave, called Marie-Joseph Angélique, who allegedly set fire to her master's Montréal house and destroyed nearly 50 homes.

As punishment, she was tortured and hanged to warn other Visual Minority slaves. No amount of apology or compensation can indeed remedy what was done during that period. Still, to feel that there is no need for it opens up old wounds all over again. In 2017, the UN Human Rights Council on people of African descent in Canada recommended that the Government of Canada apologize and consider offering reparations to African Canadians for enslavement and historical injustices. However, when reporters asked Prime Minister Justin Trudeau whether he would act on the recommendation, he didn't answer the question.

It is this kind of body language that gives the impression that the current generation could have acted the same way if they were in the position of their White ancestors. In recent times, many Canadians agree that the White-presenting people treated their Visual Minority slaves terribly. Still, once reparation comes into the discussion, it is as if a panic button is activated. People will start coming up with all sorts of arguments why that shouldn't be the case. Some argue that African Canadians are not descendants of the Visual Minority slaves in Canada. Regardless of the arguments, perhaps something should be done to show that the White-presenting people of today would have acted differently if they were in the shoes of their ancestors.

Canada's Historic Racism Dates

On August 20, 1619, Jamestown received the first shipload of enslaved Africans to arrive in British North America. An enslaved African six-year-old boy, who was sold several times, was the first enslaved African to reside in Canada. He was the property of Sir David Kirke. After he was sold several times, he was eventually bought by Father Paul Le Jeune, who baptized him as a Catholic and gave him the name Olivier Le Jeune.

Louis XIV's Code Noir code allowed slavery for economic purposes, on March 1, 1685. Four years later, King Louis XIV of France approved the request of colonists of New France to keep Pawnee Indian and Visual Minority slaves. Visual Minority slaves were the first inhabitants of Fort Pontchartrain on the shores of the Detroit River that was established by the ambitious French fur-trader and colonizer, Antoine de Lamothe Cadillac, on January 1, 1701. Eight years later, King Louis XIV formally authorized slavery when he allowed his Canadian subjects to possess slaves.

On January 1, 1790, the Imperial Statute was enacted, which allowed settlers to bring enslaved people to Upper Canada. The slave master only owes the slave food and clothing. The Chloe Cooley case on March 21, 1793, convinced Lieutenant-Governor Simcoe that slavery needed to be abolished. On January 1, 1819, Attorney General John Beverley Robinson built on the work of Simcoe by declaring Visual Minorities that reside in Canada free. He also publicly affirmed that Canadian courts would recognize and uphold this freedom. An Imperial Act abolished slavery throughout the British colonies, which became effective on August 1, 1834.

Oriental Asian Canadian Racism

African Canadians are not the only ones that have suffered from discrimination in Canada. Asians have also been subjected to racism in this nation. Asians have been living in Canada since 1788 when Chinese workers arrived in the Nuu-chah-nulth territory to establish fur trade settlements. Chinese pioneers have achieved a lot, but they have also been subjected to legislated discrimination imposed on them by past governments. The laws denied them fundamental human rights. The Chinese were attracted to the lower Fraser Valley when gold was discovered in 1857. They arrived from San Francisco by boat in Victoria.

Chinese Canadians were segregated economically, socially, and politically. An example of this is the fact that Chinese Canadians were not allowed to swim in Victoria's Crystal pool, according to consultation forum participants. By 1923, Canadian Chinese were not allowed to employ White-presenting women as waitresses in their restaurants by acts passed in British Columbia. In the long run, when this legislation was not sustainable, it paved the way for a new act that requires Chinese merchants to require a special permit to employ White-presenting women. Racial discrimination could also be seen in movie theatres where Chinese Canadians were required to sit on the balcony.

Chinese Canadians could not become professionals, such as pharmacists, lawyers, doctors, or engineers, until after 1947. Before that time, they were also not allowed to vote because their names were not on the voting list. Also, during World War II, Chinese Canadians were not allowed to be enlisted because the government was afraid that the veterans might ask for the right to vote after the war. It was the 1967 immigration reform that changed things a bit when it created a points system and eliminated racial discrimination in immigration policy. This policy led to a steady rise in Chinese immigration, especially in the 1970s and 1980s.

Henry Dundas

Henry Dundas is an icon that is synonymous with racism. He was a Scottish politician in the late 18th century. He was appointed the first Secretary of State for War in 1794. He became famous as the tyrant that fought against the abolition of slavery in the British Empire. His commitment to this evil cause led to the delay of the abolition of slavery for 15 years. The slave trade should have ended in 1792. However, because of Dundas, it ended in 1807. A year earlier, he was impeached in the United Kingdom for mishandling public funds.

He never returned to public office even though he was acquitted. The implication of the role he played in the delay of the abolition of the slave trade is that he made 630,000 people wait for more than a decade to obtain their freedom. Due to the kind of man he was in the history of racism, a petition was signed to rename Dundas Street in Toronto (and was successful in 2022). This followed the calls to tear down his statue in Edinburgh. According to the leader of the city, there would be no sense of loss if the statue was removed and replaced with another thing.

Protesters pointed out that it is shameful for Toronto to keep the name of Dundas because he didn't have any significant positive contribution to Canada. The only significant role he played was to delay the abolition of the slave trade. Interestingly, it was a descendant of Henry Dundas that urged the city to make changes to the statue of Dundas. According to him, a plaque explaining his racist history should be put in place. This inspired a movement to tear down the statue altogether.

Canadian Native Residential School System

Residential schooling was one of the colonial policies that were damaging to the indigenous people of Canada. The system was meant to eradicate the cultural beliefs, language, and spiritual beliefs of the people. These schools were attended by more than 150,000 Metis, First Nations, and Inuit children until their closure in the mid-

1990s. Government officials admitted that these schools aimed to Christianize and civilize Aboriginal children. Sadly, many children suffered sexual, physical, and psychological abuse while attending these schools. These effects caused them health problems and led some into a life of crime and substance abuse, according to the Truth and Reconciliation Commission of Canada.

Besides, many of the residential schools were severely underfunded, leading to poor living conditions and poor nutrition for the children, which led to sickness and death, according to a 2003 study. These attempts of forced assimilation were not successful due to the resistance and resilience of many indigenous communities. Still, they affected the structure and integrity of families and communities. They also led to an identity crisis for many individuals. Interestingly, researchers discovered that the traumatizing impact of residential schooling still has a way of affecting the descendants of the victims. This concept is called **historical trauma.**

As a result of historical trauma, descendants of the people that experienced the unpleasant circumstances during the residential schooling system, have poorer health status. This was discovered by a 2014 study. The study showed that the children of those whose ancestors didn't attend these schools enjoy better health status. The study showed that it is worse in families where multiple generations attended these schools. These studies imply that it is not only the people that were exposed to the trauma of attending residential schools that suffered from the impacts. Their descendants are also in danger of being affected by the experiences of their ancestors.

The terror and dehumanizing acts perpetrated in the Residential Schools can only be imagined. Indigenous Canadians have been saying for years that their children were forcefully taken from them to the schools and subjected to abuse that killed many of them. Many of the children that died during that period were buried in unmarked gravesites. A report in the New York Times in June 2021 showed that 751 unmarked gravesites of children at the site of a residential school in Saskatchewan were discovered by the Cowessess. These children were forcefully taken from their families, and they never returned to them again.

The parents kept searching and looking forward to them returning home, but it never happened. They were treasures to their families and they never stopped missing them. However, to White supremacists, they were nothing but specimens that were not resilient enough to receive civility. These children are not mere numbers. So, no one should dare to dismiss this discovery as just one of those things that happened in the past. They had names and full lives ahead of them, but they were denied by racist White supremacists.

Racial Inequity In the US

Just like Canada, the US also has a disturbing history of racism. We will explore some of them below:

Who And How Many Early Presidents Were Slave Owners

It is a common saying in the US that all men were created equal. Yet, the history of racism shows that it seems the saying should be changed into "all White men are created equal" because it was not an ideology that was practiced by many of the former presidents of the nation. At least 12 Chief Executives of all American presidents had slaves during their lifetime. Incredibly, eight of these twelve held enslaved people while they were in office! Enslaved people helped build the White House. Of all the earlier US presidents, only John Adams and his son John Quincy Adams did not own enslaved people.

George Washington had close to three hundred enslaved men in his Mount Vernon plantation. Also, Thomas Jefferson owned around 175 enslaved workers. Interestingly, during that same period, Jefferson described slavery as an "assemblage of horrors." Andre Jackson, James Monroe, and James Madison had several dozen enslaved workers. Martin Van Buren also owned a slave early in his career. Before becoming president in 1841, William Henry Harrison inherited several enslaved people. In the case of James Polk and John Tyler, they were both enslavers during their stints in office.

Zachary Taylor served as the president of America between 1849 and 1850. He was the last chief executive to have slaves while serving in office. In his plantations in Kentucky, Mississippi, and Louisiana, he had close to 150 enslaved people. Surprisingly, the last two Chief Executives that owned slaves were close associates of

Abraham Lincoln. Meanwhile, Lincoln was the man that signed the Emancipation Proclamation and championed the passage of the 13th Amendment, which ended slavery. Interestingly, the man who served as Lincoln's vice president, Andrew Johnson, had owned a dozen enslaved people.

If several American presidents were slave owners, it is not surprising that systemic racism exists in the nation today. If the White House was built by slaves, I don't expect some of the policies that are made there to be in favour of racial minorities. Former American president, Ulysses Grant, had declared that it was a stain on the Union Army that people were once traded like cattle. It is also a stain on the US that its presidents once traded human beings like animals.

Reparations For Slave Owners 1800s

The crime committed against people to enslave them was bad enough; the fact that slave owners were compensated, only made it worse. Why should the people that bought and sold human beings be entitled to any form of compensation? They used and abused these people for years, giving them only food, clothing, and shelter. Yet, they were compensated for letting them go. It doesn't make sense in any way. It shouldn't be the slave owners that should be compensated, rather, the people that were enslaved should get apologies and compensations for years of use and abuse.

In 1833, 40% of Britain's national budget was used to purchase the freedom of all slaves from the Empire. It was so bad, that the money that was borrowed for the Slavery Abolition Act was not fully paid back until 2015! Why would the government of a nation have to dig so deep into its pocket to pay slave owners? The implication of this is that the tax of people that were not born during the slave trade era was still used to pay the families of slave owners! After the British government outlawed slavery in Britain and its American possessions, 20 million pounds was paid (around 17 billion pounds today) to compensate slave owners. This is so ridiculous!

It was easy for former slave owners and their families to be compensated by the government. On the other hand, years of clamouring for reparations for slaves by the Visual Minority community have fallen on deaf ears. At some point, each freed family was given forty acres of tillable land in the Sea Islands and around Charleston, South Carolina. However, it was reversed by President Andrew Johnson after the assassination of Abraham Lincoln. It is not shocking because Johnson was a former slave owner. Until now, there has not been any form of notable compensation for the family of freed slaves.

Violent Crimes Committed Against Slaves

For trying to escape or being caught learning to read, violent crimes were committed against slaves. Slaves in the northernmost Southern states had better working conditions. However, those in Deep South plantations were subjected to harsh conditions. They were usually subjected to degradation, brutality, and inhumanity. Executions, whippings, and rapes were commonplace. They were denied educational opportunities, including the right to read or write. Some states also prohibited slaves from holding religious gatherings because they feared that such meetings could facilitate insurrection or escape. The situation got worse in 1831 after the rebellion of Nat Turner.

Slave women were often victims of sexual rape and sexual abuse. Many that fought back these abuses, lost their lives in the process. During this period, women, whether White or Black, were generally treated as property or chattels by the patriarchal Southern culture of that era. So, it only made things worse and more complicated for slave women. As a result of the adoption of the *partus sequitur ventrem* into Virginia law in 1662, any child born due to sexual relations between any man and a Visual Minority woman was regarded as a slave regardless of race and status of the father.

The product of this terrible legislation was several generations of mulatto or mixed-race slaves. As a result of this, southern societies in the US strongly prohibited sexual relations between White-presenting women and Visual Minority men, to preserve their "racial purity." An 1850 publication taught slave owners to produce the ideal slave by implementing the following:

- Instill fear in the minds of slaves

- Teach the servants to take an interest in the master's enterprise

- Maintain strict discipline and "unconditional submission"

- Create a sense of personal inferiority, so slaves "know their place"

- Ensure that the slave is uneducated, helpless, and dependent by depriving them of access to education and recreation.

Story Of Emmett Till and Similarities To Story Of George Floyd

In August 1955, Emmett Till, a 14-year-old boy from Chicago, was lynched while visiting his family in Money, Mississippi. What was his crime? It was claimed that he was whistling at a White woman. A group of White-presenting men kidnapped him, tortured him, and eventually killed him. When his body was discovered in the Tallahatchie River, it had a 4-pound cotton gin fan barb-wired to the neck. Two men were arrested regarding the case but were acquitted on a murder charge and were also not indicted for kidnapping. Years later, the woman involved in the case claimed that she lied when she said that Till had offended her.

Till's mother decided to force the world to take a deeper look into racism in the US when she decided to take the bold step of a public, open-casket viewing. For four days, thousands of people stood in line to view the murdered body of the teenager at the South Side at Roberts Temple Church of God in Christ, 4021 S. State St. She also allowed the press to photograph her son's mutilated remains and circulate the image in newspapers and magazines. Till's death and the action of his mother inspired a generation of Americans to end Jim Crow segregation and initiated a nine-year battle that led to the passage of the Civil Rights Act.

There is a similarity between the death of Till and George Floyd. Black Lives Matter protesters are hoping that Floyd's death could have a similar impact on racism in America. Many protesters chanted Till's name in response to the death of Floyd. Sadly, there have been several Visual Minorities that have been killed by White-presenting people for flimsy reasons just like these two. However, the deaths of these two were the points of clarity where the pain of Visual Minority people could be articulated to White-presenting people.

Black Wall Street 1921 Cover-Up Race Massacre

In 1921, a violent White mob destroyed a prosperous Visual Minority neighborhood in Tulsa, Okla. It was indeed a sad event that destroyed years of Visual Minority success. It involved the destruction of over 1250 homes and led to the death of hundreds of residents. It was an event that reminds us all that there are so many White-presenting people that cannot stand the success of Visual Minority people. As hundreds of people were killed and homes were destroyed, the hope of reducing the wealth gap in the US went with it.

Before the incident in May 1921, the neighborhood of Greenwood in Tulsa, Okla., was the antidote to the racial oppression of those times. It was the haven built in the early part of the century by Visual Minority people for Visual Minority people. It had around 10,000 residents and it was a thriving commercial community where

Visual Minority people could live, work, learn, shop, play, and worship freely. It was so successful that it was called America's Black Wall Street.

However, the sheer success of this community angered some people and they felt that it deserved to be ravaged by flames. This incident is a reminder of how easy it is to destroy what has been built for years. In less than twenty-four hours of violence, many were sent to early graves and a thriving community of Visual Minority people came crashing to the earth. What was the offense of these people? They were thriving and achieving success although they were Visual Minorities. For people who don't think racism exists, this incident should make them think twice. It happened in 1921, which was not that long ago.

The 21st Century Implications of the Tuskegee Syphilis Study

This study is one of the greatest damages to the trust of African Americans in the American public health system and the Federal Government. This is because it reinforced the belief that the government doesn't value the lives of Visual Minority Americans like it does White Americans. It is also one of the reasons Visual Minority Americans didn't seek treatment for AIDS in the 1980s and the longstanding fear of vaccination. In this study, African Americans were the participants. The number of participants is estimated to have been around 76 and 111.

All of them were men who had syphilis when they were enrolled in the study. They were not treated because the researchers were trying to understand the natural course of untreated syphilis. The participants were recruited with the false promise that they would be given free treatment. However, they were never treated, even when penicillin became available as the treatment for the disease. These men had trusted the doctors, but they never knew that they were nothing but guinea pigs to them.

Sadly, the findings from the study were published from 1936 until the early 1970s. The experiment didn't stop until 1972 when the accounts of the study appeared in the national press. By this time, between 28 and 100 of the participants had died of advanced syphilis. The US government paid $10 million as compensation and President Clinton offered a public apology to the participants on behalf of the Federal Government. Yet, many African Americans cannot understand why doctors didn't question the ethicality of the study all through the period it was published.

Why was it that no one did anything about it until it went public in the national press? If the participants were White, would the case have ended with an apology and payment of compensation to the survivors, or would more drastic actions have been taken? It seems no one did anything about it because these men were Visual Minorities who (at the time) had low social status. The experiment had to end, and the government took steps to prevent being disgraced in the international community. This kind of incident makes me wonder what exactly the worth of the lives of Visual Minority people in America is.

Chapter Thirteen:
Advanced Racist History From The
1700s To Modern Day

Perhaps, the pain of Visual Minority people over so many years is becoming much clearer to you by now, after some of the things we explored in the last chapter. We will continue in this chapter to ensure that no one has any reasons to see racism as something that can be swept under the carpet any longer.

Racist Slave History Is Recent

Racist slave history didn't end that long ago. It only ended a few generations ago. This is within my great-grandparents' lifetime. If you were born in the 1950s to the 1970s, this period may apply to you in the way it applies to me. Although all the northern states of the US abolished slavery between 1774 and 1804, the institution remained in the southern states, which eventually led to the civil war. The northern states' economy does not depend on forced labor due to their advancement in technology and industrialization. So, it was easy for them to abolish slavery and speak against it.

They described it as a sin and also believed that it is regressive and inefficient. On the other hand, the southern states heavily relied on it because of their tobacco and cotton plantations. The high demand for cotton in the UK due to the industrialization of the textile industry only intensified the need of the southern states to produce more cotton. Meanwhile, cotton production requires the use of hands in the separation of the seeds. So, the southern states relied heavily on the assistance of enslaved Africans to help sustain this industry that was their main economy. As a result of this, they were not willing to abolish slavery.

The US congress outlawed slavery in 1808 but the institution continued to flourish domestically in the southern states. By 1860, more than 4 million enslaved Africans were living in the southern states, especially on the plantation farms. They had formed one-third of the population. These slaves were getting married and had children in bondage, which increased their population. There was no legal basis for this, but the slave owners encouraged the act for various reasons. It increased the number of slaves they had, and it also made it more difficult for the slaves to escape. Many of them chose to keep their family over their freedom.

The movement to abolish slavery in America gained strength between the 1830s and the 1860s. It was led by free Visual Minority slaves, such as Frederick Douglass and White supporters, such as William Lloyd Garrison and Harriet Beecher Stowe. Antislavery northerners and free Visual Minority people started helping enslaved people to escape from southern plantations via a loose network of safe houses to the north. This practice was known as the **Underground Railroad**. This movement helped close to 100,000 enslaved people to attain freedom. The success of the Underground Railroad further fueled antislavery sentiment in the north.

The Civil War between 1861 and 1865 was a necessary evil that strengthened the resolve to end slavery in America. Lincoln's Emancipation declaration freed close to three million enslaved people, which deprived the southern states of the labor force. However, this didn't put an end to slavery in the US. The struggle continued with the 13th, 14th, and 15th Amendments. Even at that, a significant breakthrough in racial equality between Visual Minorities and White-presenting people was not achieved constitutionally until the Civil Rights Movement of the 1960s.

Because the history of racism and slavery in America is still very recent, we should not be surprised that some of its legacies and impacts are still in full force today. Of course, it is no longer explicit and the American and Canadian constitution does not legitimize it. Still, the gulf in separation is there for anyone observant to see. Many continue to harbor the resentment and sentiments of their ancestors against Visual Minority people. Indeed, we have come very far but the battle is far from over.

Real Historical Accounts Of Christopher Columbus And Pocahontas

Due to the way Disney presented the story of Pocahontas, many Americans don't know the real story. Just like many stories around the history of the US, Pocahontas has been "whitened," romanticized and rebranded. Many see her as the Native American woman who united two cultures. Many also see her as the savior of Captain John Smith. Indeed, there are elements of truth in the story. However, many of the elements that defined the ugly side of American history have been removed to make it appealing. The true historical account of Pocahontas is the story behind America's exploitation of the Native Americans in the New World.

It all began with Christopher Columbus' search for more territories, which led the European settlers to Powhatan land intending to colonize Jamestown. Pocahontas was born around 1595. She was the daughter of the ruler of the Powhatan tribal nation. Her birth name was Amonute and she went by the name Matoaka. She probably hid her real name from the Europeans because her people believed that the Europeans would hurt them if they knew their real names. In May 1607, the first English settlers arrived in the Jamestown colony. Pocahontas' brother kidnapped colonist Captain John Smith that winter.

After making a spectacle of him in front of several Powhatan tribes, he took him to Chief Powhatan. Smith claimed that his head was placed on two stones and his head was about to be smashed by a warrior when Pocahontas rushed to save him by placing her head on his own. However, this is hotly debated because Powhatan culture has this kind of ceremony. So, Smith might have misunderstood the people and felt he was in peril. Anyway, Chief Powhatan bartered with Smith after that, which began an often-strained relationship between the colonists and the Indians.

Pocahontas would become an important Powhatan emissary known to the colonists. She helped in the release of Powhatan prisoners and occasionally brought food to the hungry European settlers. By 1609, the colonists were increasingly dependent on the Powhatan for their survival because they were ravaged by disease, drought, and starvation. They began to threaten to burn Powhatan towns for food because they were desperate and dying. So, Chief Powhatan suggested bartering with Captain Smith but negotiation broke down. To protect his people, the chief planned an ambush and Smith's execution. However, it didn't succeed because Pocahontas informed Smith about her father's plan.

Later on, Smith got injured and returned to England, but Pocahontas and her father were told that he was dead. She avoided the English after that until she was lured into their ship by Captain Samuel Argall and kidnapped in 1613 during the First Anglo-Powhatan War. Argall told the chief that he would not return her unless her father returned stolen weapons, released English prisoners, and sent them food. To their surprise and Pocahontas dismay, the chief only sent half of the ransom. She was not released and when she found out that her father was not willing to send the whole ransom for her, it prompted her to be more open to learning the culture of the English and learned about Christianity.

She eventually converted to Christianity and was baptized and given the name "Rebecca." She met a widower and tobacco planter, John Rolfe, during her imprisonment. She eventually married him after the

Virginia governor, Sir Thomas Dale, and Pocahontas' father consented to the marriage. The marriage improved the relations between the colonists and the Indians. In the bid to get financial support, Sir Thomas Dale took Pocahontas and some Powhatan Indians, in 1613, to England to convince the British government about the success of their mission in Jamestown. Pocahontas was revered as a princess in London and even met the royal family.

Surprisingly, she met Captain Smith there. He wasn't dead and she called him "father" when she saw that he was still alive and reportedly rebuked him for his treatment of her people. On her way back to Virginia in March 1617, she became gravely ill and eventually died. She had a son with John Rolfe before her death. So, in reality, the story of Pocahontas is the story of the exploitation and perceived supremacy of European White-presenting people over Powhatan Indians. It is the story of years of trying to destroy another culture to establish a new one.

Nazis Modelled Racism After Pre/Post USA Civil War Segregation History

One of the greatest, if not the greatest crime in the history of humanity is the Holocaust. Many would agree, it was one of the times humans descended from the height of civility to the depth of barbarism. It is indeed an everlasting shock. However, Hitler's mindset and crime can be linked to America's pre/post-civil war segregation history. In other words, Hitler was inspired by America's racism. What is the link? Many aspects of

American society appealed to the Nazis, including Hollywood production values, the culture of the sport, and the mythology of the Frontier. Hitler approvingly remarked that the White settlers in America had "gunned down the millions of redskins to a few hundred thousand."

America was what he had in mind when he spoke of *Lebensraum*, the German drive for "living space" in Eastern Europe. In "Mein Kampf," Hitler spoke in glowing terms about how America is one of the leading nations in terms of a primarily racial conception of citizenship, by preventing certain races from naturalization. Many Americans might be uncomfortable with the fact that the Nazis cited American precedents. Still, the resemblance could not have been more striking in some ways. For example, the enslavement of African Americans was written into the US Constitution.

To make it worse, Thomas Jefferson boldly spoke about the need to "extirpate" or "eliminate" Native Americans! An Oregonian settler wrote in 1856, "Extermination, however unchristian-like it may appear, seems to be the only resort left for the protection of life and property." General Philip Sheridan did not mince words either when he spoke about "annihilation, obliteration, and destruction." Indeed, the federal policies of the US didn't mandate the physical annihilation of Native Americans. Yet, somehow, this population reduced from millions to around two hundred thousand between 1500 and 1900! How do you explain or justify that?

Meanwhile, as all of this was going on, Hitler was taking note. He observed how America has a knack for maintaining an air of questionable innocence in the wake of mass death, and he had a blueprint for his massacre of the Jews. In the early months of the Soviet Union invasion, Hitler made frequent mention of the American West. He said Volga would be "our Mississippi," and "Europe—and not America—will be the land of unlimited possibilities." Hitler's regime spoke admirably about American race law. Whether we fail to see it or not, Jim Crow laws in the American South were the precedent for the Nazi's justification for racial discrimination and annihilation.

Reparations To Slave Owners In The US And Canada

Long after the slave trade was abolished in the UK, it took some years before the slaves could be freed because slave owners demanded compensation from the government before they could let go of their "properties." This was the case also in the US and Canada. In the US, President Lincoln signed the District of Columbia Emancipation Act in April 1862. This act outlawed slavery in the District, which mandated its 900 slaveholders let go of their slaves. However, this would not happen without the federal government paying $300 per slave. This is worth $8,000 in 2020.

Canada's first prime minister, Sir John Macdonald, also had a family connection to the slave trade. His father-in-law, Thomas James Bernard, was among the slave owners that were generously compensated by the British government for releasing slaves. He lived in Jamaica, where he had a sugar plantation and had 96 slaves. As a result, he received £1,723 from the government during this period. This is a lot of money even at that time when you consider the fact that the annual salary of a skilled worker during that period was £60. Among those that were compensated by the British government, apart from Bernard, 31 others had ties to Canada.

For example, merchant Robert Neilson of Hamilton owned 568 slaves in Trinidad, which entitled him to £28,763 in compensation. Sir Thomas John Cochrane, who was the governor of Newfoundland between 1825 and 1834, owned 72 slaves. Unlike the others, his request for over £3,000 in compensation was rejected. When you consider the fact that several US presidents had slaves and some founding prime ministers of Canada owned slaves, it becomes obvious that both nations were deeply entrenched in racism until they started shedding off this barbaric treatment of fellow human beings, in recent times.

Even at the time of releasing the slaves, they still saw them as their property that should not be taken away from them, without compensation. This shows the perception of these people of Visual Minority people. The terrible and dehumanizing practice of slavery might have ended, but the perception of Visual Minority people as inferior human beings will not go away that easily.

Treatment Of Slaves By White Masters

Slavery is unnatural. So, it was not surprising that slaves often resisted their masters in various ways. Sometimes, they could slow down their work or pretend to be sick when their masters don't treat them well. Some stole food from their masters because their food ration was usually insufficient to withstand the rigors of physical labor. To keep them in check, there were measures such as cutting off their limbs. Branding, whipping, and severing of the Achilles tendon were also common ways of making some slaves a deterrent to others, to keep them in perpetual subjection to their masters.

It was critical for the slave masters to prevent slaves from being enlightened, to keep them in line. To ensure this, slave masters often made sure that enslaved people were not allowed any form of education. They were punished severely whenever caught reading or writing. James Ramsay was a doctor that worked for several sugar plantations in St Kitts. In his book, *Essay on the Treatment and Conversion of African Slaves in the British Sugar Colonies* (1784), he wrote about his shock concerning the treatment of slaves by their masters. He noticed that the punishment for crimes such as eating the sugar cane, absence from work, neglect, and theft, included beating with a stick, sometimes to the breaking of bones.

It could also include cart whipping, placing an iron crook around the neck, a ring about the ankle, slitting of ears, and confinement to the dungeon. In some instances, slaves lost their eyes due to a beating and some were even castrated. In the words of Ramsay, slavery wasn't a place where words such as decency, morality, or sympathy existed. Rather, it was the place of oppression and punitive measures that shortened the lives of the enslaved people. Sadly, the constitution empowered slave masters to do whatever they wanted to the slaves. They were helpless in the hands of people who treated them worse than animals.

States that had a large number of slaves introduced slave codes to ensure that slaves were under the tight control of their masters. Slaves could be killed for various reasons, including rape, arson, burglary, assault of a White person, and murder. Plantation owners believed that these punishments were necessary to ensure that slaves would never think about rebelling or escaping.

Black Slaves' Involvement In The Civil War

The American Civil War played a vital role in conferring citizenship on Visual Minorities. It was an opportunity to serve the nation and prove that they deserved to be recognized as American citizens. When Visual Minorities volunteered to be enlisted in the Union Army, they were turned down initially because of a Federal law dating from 1792 that prevented Negroes from bearing arms for the US army. Volunteers in Boston protested the decision, and this made President Lincoln rethink the decision. Besides, the declining number of White volunteers and the escalating number of former slaves forced his hand.

Congress passed the Second Confiscation and Militia Act in July 1862, which freed slaves who had masters in the Confederate Army. This effectively abolished slavery in the US territories. Visual Minority recruitment into the army was pursued in earnest after the Emancipation Proclamation was publicly announced. However, recruitment was slow until Visual Minority leaders such as Frederick Douglass encouraged Visual Minorities to take advantage of the opportunity to gain full citizenship. By the end of the Civil War, over 179,000 Visual Minority men served as soldiers, with nearly 40,000 of them dying during the war. They also served in non-combat roles such as carpentry, cooking, and as surgeons.

Still, they faced prejudice in the US army. Visual Minority soldiers were initially paid $7 per month while their White counterparts earned $13. Congress granted equal pay to the troops in June 1864 and the Visual Minority soldiers also started receiving comparable medical care. However, the Visual Minority troops faced greater peril than the White troops. When captured, Visual Minority soldiers often faced more severe punishment than White soldiers. For example, Visual Minority soldiers that were captured at the Fort Pillow, TN, engagement in 1864 were shot dead by Confederate soldiers and Confederate General Nathan B. Forrest did nothing to stop the massacre.

The difficulty of Visual Minority People To Close The Wealth Gap

The Emancipation Proclamation was supposed to end the wage gap between Visual Minorities and White families in the US. It was assumed that institutionalized slavery was the reason Visual Minorities were entrenched in poverty. However, the difference has not been significant since the end of slavery. In 1863, 1% of the national wealth belonged to Visual Minority Americans. As of 2020, it is 1.5%. It is quite difficult to explain the reason for the stagnation after the end of slavery and the achievements of civil rights. Still, the people in power have found subtle ways to thwart the economic promise of emancipation.

In their bid to search for high wages in the urban industry, millions of Visual Minority families moved from the South, but the gap has still not closed since then. The solution was supposed to be simple. Visual Minorities should get educated, move into the city, and acquire skills. However, the gap has refused to vanish. Ta-Nehisi Coates calls this myth "the quiet plunder." People in power have found a way to create discriminatory economic policies that ensures that nothing has changed despite freedom and civil rights. In the words of Visual Minority mathematician and sociologist, Kelly Miller, in 1930, "The Negro is up against the White man's standard without the White man's opportunities."

As Visual Minority people moved from the South, they found themselves in neighborhoods where landlords demand high rents, and they accepted the terms due to a lack of alternatives. Despite the efforts of Visual Minority people by training up, joining unions, and saving, Southern Democrats were gatekeepers of New Deal legislation, and they ensured that they built in White privilege when the federal government created economic entitlements, according to Calvin Schermerhorn of the Washington Post. African Americans seeking home loans were deemed ineligible because the government wouldn't guarantee the loans. This and other racist schemes have ensured that Visual Minorities have kept striving since the end of slavery and civil rights but have not achieved anywhere near their White counterparts.

Chapter Fourteen:
My Perspectives

I have spent most parts of the last three chapters exploring facts around racism. Based on these facts and my perspectives, I will point out some things that I feel are necessary as we continue this discussion in this chapter.

Focal Point Compared

Growing up with White-presenting and Visual Minority people, I sometimes felt Caucasians focused more on what I do vocationally than who I was personally when getting to know me. By contrast, Visual Minority people focused more on who I was personally, rather than what I did for a living. Of course, it is not every White-presenting person that I met that had this approach. Still, most of them did. Why should what I do for a living matter to them, more than who I am as an individual? I guess it was their way of deciding whether they should treat me with respect or not.

Most likely, they may have been considering the perceptions they have been given by their parents and other White-presenting people around them, about Visual Minority people. They are trying to find out whether those preconceived notions are right or not. The danger of this kind of approach, when getting to know people, is that you would rate them and judge them based on criteria that can change. I might not have a high-paying job today but that doesn't mean that it will always be like that. In my mind, people should be more concerned about my worldview and abilities. My character and the way I treat people should come first, before any discussion about what I do for a living.

It is better to have a low-profile friend who would treat you with respect and be there for you, than a high-profile friend that doesn't care about you and would dump you when things are not going your way. You don't have to be a White-presenting or Visual Minority to show virtues such as empathy, respect, affection, and loyalty. Sadly, some people around me tend to judge a book by its cover. They get carried away by the kind of job you have and your social status, forgetting the more important things that make friendship and family work.

I often notice the disapproval based on first impressions. It usually takes more time before they get to know me better and make better judgments about me. Some of them end up admitting that they were wrong about me. They confess that they had thought I would be inconsiderate and difficult to like based on their first impression. I wouldn't blame them too much. They are simply acting based on the information they have at their disposal. This is why I believe that racism can be resolved if more White-presenting people have Visual Minority people as their friends and family.

It is always a different ball game when you get closer to people. No one should judge people based on their appearance. Sadly, skin color is enough to give people the wrong impression and perception of a person. Sometimes it feels Visual Minorities have to prove to White-presenting people all over again that they are harmless while White-presenting people get the benefit of the doubt until they prove otherwise. This shouldn't be happening in the modern world but that feels like the reality of the situation at the moment.

Assertiveness Vs Endurance

I get angry sometimes, which was especially the case in my teenage years because then, I felt there was no one I could talk to about both my White-presenting and Visual Minority families (because no one was as ethnically unique as I was). In my teens, I used to think, why do Caucasians argue so much, and Visual Minority people endure so much? This was the recurrent theme around me at the time. White-presenting people often feel entitled and are never afraid to express themselves. They never have to feel that their opinion would not matter. This doesn't mean that no one counters their opinion. Still, they were assertive and felt that they could always say whatever they wanted.

On the other hand, the Visual Minority people around me are often careful before they speak. They usually have to think twice and ensure that their opinion made sense before they aired it. I couldn't understand what was keeping them from expressing themselves as freely as the White-presenting people around me. I got to understand by observing the theme of their discussions. I noticed that when Visual Minorities say something, he or she usually has to be ready to offer a logical defense of that opinion before it can be accepted as a valid claim. They must be ready to face the kind of scrutiny Caucasians don't face.

So, when they are not ready to offer further explanations to an initial claim, they would rather keep quiet. The White-presenting people around me don't face that same kind of challenge. Even when they say things that don't make sense, they are pointed out without the kind of suspicion that I usually observe when Visual Minority people speak. It seems that it is assumed that you are intelligent when you are White-presenting and may have the propensity for folly when you are a Visual Minority. Therefore, it is the norm when a White person says sensible things, but it is an unexpected situation when a Visual Minority says something intelligent.

I realized that the Visual Minority people around me had realized the biased treatment. So, they got used to not saying so much unless they felt that it was necessary to speak. They got tired of the extra effort and energy they have to exert when making their point. Speaking sometimes feels like walking on eggshells, whenever they are speaking when White-presenting people are around. I noticed that the situation is never the same when only Visual Minority people are involved in a conversation. I observed the air of confidence they radiate when they have discussions involving only Visual Minority people.

I believe that the confrontation and scrutiny that White-presenting people displayed around me were subconscious. Whenever anyone pointed out that Visual Minority people face more criticism and have to do more to convince them that they are making a valid point, unlike a White person, they denied it affirmatively. Yet, in my experience, it is obvious that the playing field is not level when having conversations about race with one another. To me, White-presenting people seemed more assertive, while Visual Minority people often struggle to articulate. Many Visual Minority people may not feel free to point out that they are being treated differently.

Constant Questioning

I get asked where I'm from all the time by people I hardly know. I kept wondering if that happens to everybody. Why does it even matter? Doesn't the fact that I live in a nation be enough to show anyone that I am from that country? The fact that I get asked shows me that people believe that I am not from Canada even though I have lived in the nation all my life.

It is one thing to say something when under the pressure of saying something politically correct or socially acceptable; it is another thing to say what you think. Think about it; when you see White-presenting people in these countries, does it ever cross your mind to ask them where they are from?

I asked my White-presenting friends this question and it became obvious to them that they were asking the wrong questions that are racially inclined. On some days when I am curious, I ask White-presenting people I meet where they are from. It is sometimes awkward for them. They feel that it should have been obvious to me that they are citizens of the nation. It often looks as though I saw a Zebra and I couldn't recognize it. Like I said earlier, many of them treat Visual Minority people differently, subconsciously. It is almost like a reflex action.

The thing about subconscious actions is that you wouldn't be able to hide them, no matter how hard you try. Your body language would give you away at some point. Visual Minority people have done so much to prove that they love their nation as much as White-presenting people. From the days of fighting in the Civil War, among other heroic actions, Visual Minority people have shown that they love their country and would die for it when necessary. Sadly, some White-presenting people are quick to remind them that they are second-class citizens, in overt and covert ways.

It is never comfortable when someone reminds you that you are not a Canadian, American, or British because you have Visual Minority ancestors. Of course, it is not as though I am not proud of my minority ancestry. Still, it is not a question I am comfortable answering, especially when I am meeting a person for the first time. If a friend that I have known for years asks me out of curiosity, that would be a different situation. It is awkward when someone I meet for the first time asks me where I am 'originally' from.

Different Treatment

I also notice this difference in treatment when I take my dog off a leash. Before I take my dog off a leash, I look to see if White-presenting people have done so first. There are many reasons I do this. One of them is that I don't want to answer questions about my ethnicity because it is one of the ways I get to meet a lot of strangers. The last thing I want is to be emotionally disturbed because of the questions someone is asking me about my unidentifiable ethnicity when I am taking my dog off a leash.

At that moment, I just want to relax and take my mind off any issue that can affect my mood. I wish some people would mind their own business but many never do. Of course, I am not against making new friends. Still, I am not comfortable with starting a friendship on the wrong note. I prefer people who would treat me with respect from the onset. When I meet you for the first time, it puts me off when one of the first questions you ask me is about my ethnicity. I wouldn't like to continue the conversation after that.

Another reason I prefer to take my dog off a leash when White-presenting people are not there is that I am more comfortable when I don't feel like they are looking at me. Some White-presenting people have this terrible culture of looking at you as a Visual Minority as though you are not meant to be there. I usually try my best to focus on what I am doing and ignore any prying eyes. However, the reality is that it is easier said than done. I don't want the mental torture and emotional strain of trying to be perfect because I feel that someone is watching me and trying to see what I am doing.

It is never comfortable to be in that kind of situation or have that feeling. It feels like a strict supervisor who is doing all he can to find fault, is watching you. It gets worse when White cops are around. I am no longer at rest. I know that I am an easy target because of my skin color. That is the worst time to do anything wrong because I know that they would have valid and legit reasons to mistreat me, all in the name of "just doing their job."

Why don't White-presenting people have this same experience? Of course, I am jealous of them, sometimes. I am not ashamed of my skin color, but I wish I have the same feeling and freedom to do my thing as they have. I want to be able to go wherever I want as a law-abiding citizen, without the fear that someone is trying to watch my steps and find reasons to attack me or subject me to any form of abuse.

Ethnicity In Job Application

The feeling that I belong to a minority or inferior race, rears its ugly head again when I apply for a job. The fact that ethnicity is categorized is just not right. Someone might say that the same goes for gender. However, it is understandable that a company is interested in the gender of a potential employee because gender differences exist. I mean, there are factors such as pregnancy that have to be considered so that the organization will know how to prepare and plan for the employee. On the other hand, racial differences exist.

Of course, people are from different cultural backgrounds. However, in the context of hiring a person for a job, a person's race does not have any way of interfering or enhancing his or her ability to perform as expected. It could have been assumed that it has no meaning, and the employees are only trying to achieve inclusion. However, several studies have proven that this is not the case. It has been confirmed that people from minority races that use gimmicks to present as White have higher chances of employment.

It feels like when Aladdin knew that he would never get the chance to marry Princess Jasmine because he was not a prince. He had to pretend to be a Prince to get the chance to show his qualities, just like other suitors that were trying to get the attention of the princess and the approval of the Sultan. Other princes were judged based on their character, but he was judged based on his status in society. Meanwhile, he had the qualities that would make him a good husband for the princess. This is the kind of dilemma many Visual Minority people face today.

Many of them have the qualities that are needed for a job, but they would not get the opportunity unless they pretend that they are White. White-presenting people are judged based on the value they can add to the organization but Visual Minority people are first judged based on their skin color. Just like Aladdin, some of them lie that they are White or add White names to their resume to get a chance. This is the same problem many Mixed freelancers face today. Despite their talent and capabilities, many of them struggle to be given the chance to show what they can do when they use their real profiles.

To their dismay, they start getting job offers when they forge White profiles. They would do perfect jobs, which they would have done even if they used their real names and pictures. Sadly, we live in a world where it is assumed that you would deliver low-grade, poor-quality jobs just because you are a Visual Minority. Many Visual Minority people want to be real and present themselves to others and let them see them for who they are but what do you do when people assume that you are dumb just because you are not White?

Lack Of Exposure

Toronto is seen as so racially progressive but it's not as many people think it is. In my world, including around my father's White friends, most of the White-presenting people I know don't have and have never had Visual Minority people as confiding friends, bosses, professors, family doctors, etc. This is one of the reasons they don't know what to expect from Visual Minority people.

When people are not exposed to some things or some set of people, they only have assumptions about them. Sadly, these assumptions might be wrong because they may be based on conjectures and not facts. Sometimes, I wonder if Visual Minority people are like aliens to some White-presenting people. Some White-presenting people have never had reasons to work with Visual Minority people or speak to them. So, for some, whatever idea they have about Visual Minority people are based on second-hand experiences.

Sadly, this lack of exposure has done a lot of damage to many of such White-presenting people because it has not helped them to get the right perception of Visual Minority people. Many of them assume that Visual Minority people are aggressive and lack empathy. So, whenever they get the chance to meet Visual Minority people, they are careful. I remain optimistic it might not be too late to close this gap in this generation. Still, if the White-presenting people that have met nice Visual Minority people are willing to speak up more, it would help.

Perception By Security Operatives

Racial discrimination can be seen when a White-presenting person explores a new place or property and when a Visual Minority does the same. When it is a White-presenting person, they may be considered lost by security. On the other hand, when a Visual Minority explores a new place, they may be considered to be trespassing. Why? I see this double standard a lot and it is disheartening. Could it be possible that a person explores a new place to carry out criminal activities? Sure. It is okay to be security conscious to limit the malicious activities of criminals.

Still, it is a problem when the same yardstick is not used when profiling who could be a criminal and who couldn't.

Of course, you should expect that people would be watching you and will want to know your intention when you are new in a place. They would want to know whether you live there or you have a relative you have come to visit there. However, something is not right when you get the benefit of the doubt when you are a White person, but it may be assumed that you are a criminal when your skin is dark.

I have observed this double standard and it is just disappointing. I don't have issues with being questioned about my intention when exploring a new place, but I am not happy with the fact that I don't see White-presenting people being exposed to the same kind of scrutiny. Criminality doesn't have color. Anyone can be a criminal regardless of their gender or race. Why is that simple fact so difficult for many people to accept?

Chapter Fifteen:
My Insights

Over the years, I have discovered as a Visual Minority that I can recognize when I am in a racist situation just by listening to my instincts. I have been intellectually oblivious to it many times because I like to give people the benefit of the doubt until they prove otherwise. In this chapter, I will share my insights on identifying a racist situation, how it feels, and other issues regarding how racism came to the fore.

How Do You Know You Are In A Racist Situation?

How do you know when you're in a racist situation? It is when an unfair situation makes you feel uncomfortable that you can't fully explain, and it feels like someone is dismissing or condescending without knowing you. My theory for identifying racism through feeling racism involves the use of instincts we all have. When you feel that you are in a social situation you can't articulate and it feels like you're being stared at, you might be in a racist situation. The annoying thing about a racist situation is that you may not know what you need to do to stop the unpleasant situation. Things can happen fast and unexpectedly. You cannot control what people do, you can only control how you respond and process the situation.

This is not advice, but a trick I use in extreme cases with such people sometimes, by casually and humorously questioning them about possibly being racist, while smiling at them. When you tell them that they would have treated you differently if you were White-presenting, it feels as though they had been hit by a bullet. They would start acting like a snail trying to withdraw into its shell. They would do all they can to produce all the evidence that proves that they are not racists. Some of them could even claim that they have Visual Minority relatives and friends to convince you that they were only acting that way towards you because you did something wrong.

However, deep down, they know that they were acting that way towards you because of your skin color. Sadly, this is the kind of situation a Visual Minority in the US or Canada could be facing almost every day. Out of nowhere, someone is subtly denying you access to something for reasons you cannot explain. However, the situation changes when it is the turn of a White-presenting person. Beyond striving for excellence to be the best possible you can be as a Visual Minority, you also have to put up with many doors that are politically correctly slammed in your face because of the color of your skin.

Costly Assumptions

Some assumptions are not correct that should be addressed. For example, not every White person is ignorantly racist, and not every Visual Minority appears threatening. You must know the difference between the two. Take the sixth sense test and recognize where there is anti-racist curiosity and accept the imperfect opportunity for dialogue. There are indeed White-presenting people who use racial slang and slurs without understanding the implication. They are not trying to hurt you when they say such things or act in such ways. I am not trying to create excuses for their unacceptable behavior, still, the fact remains, that it is not every White-presenting person that uses racial slang who is trying to hurt a Visual Minority.

However, in some cases, some White-presenting people are deliberately racist. They know what they are doing when they use racial slurs and slang. They have a White supremacist mindset, and they are not ashamed to express it. Whenever they have the opportunity, they will make a Visual Minority feel that he or she is not on their level and should not be treated as equals, based on skin color. Being educated and enlightened can only do little for such people. For such individuals, studying the history of slavery and racism only inspires them more to treat Visual Minority people with disrespect.

I mean, for such people, observing what happened to Visual Minority people during the slavery era only gives them more reasons why Visual Minority people should not be respected. The prevailing mindset among White-presenting people during the slavery era was that Visual Minority people were barbarians who needed the civility and culture of White-presenting people to act acceptably. Whenever slaves revolted and killed White-presenting people, it gave them more reasons to consolidate that fact. These people forgot that slavery was not natural. You forcefully took people from their homes and families and placed them under servitude, and you expect them not to revolt?

Theory To The Origins Of Modern Day Racism In North America

Europeans were far ahead of the rest of the western world in terms of civilization. They had a modern world because they built roads and other inventions that made life easier. The British modified much of the civil processes they learned from the Romans to serve them and took over their modern world because they built firearms and loaded them on ships and the belts of soldiers who were called explorers in search of gold that they would steal from other countries. When that wasn't available, they would take slaves to build equity by saving on the cost of paying staff wages.

The British did not enjoy being under the thumb of the Romans and they found a way to overcome their oppression but then, after being whipped, started whipping by owning slaves. This behavior was duplicated by the North American colonials (also known as founding members of Canada and the US) who were

British that overcame their British oppressors. However, they too (after being oppressively whipped) started doing the oppressive whipping to Visual Minority people and here we have the beginnings of racism in the last few hundred years (only about four generations ago). This is a fact that needs to be emphasized – racism in North America started recently.

Romans were not racist but bullied Britannia. After the invention of firearms and during their search to steal gold from other countries and enslave people to avoid paying wages by force of using firearms, Britannia eventually became the bullies to North America by sending settlers that became the Canadian White-presenting people and American colonial White-presenting people. These colonial White-presenting people refused to rejoin Britain as they fought and won the battle against their fatherland to stay in North America, where they became the new bullies to local and enslaved Visual Minority people, which gave rise to the systemic racism we experience in North America today.

These North American White colonials modified their British systems to serve their new way of life without including the input of Visual Minority people. Systems of wealth, education, law, medicine, and the military were all adjusted to serve White-presenting people, which gave rise to the wealth/education gap and a strong reason White-presenting people historically do not know the Visual Minority people as friends and equals. This is where the White entitlement mindset sprang from. White-presenting people believe that they are the reason

America and Canada are developed nations today. Visual Minority people have historically been their slaves and part of the minority. So, even though slavery has been abolished, many of them still struggle to see Visual Minority people as equals.

The Plague To Be Avoided

Something I have noticed with certain White-presenting people is that they try as much as possible to avoid discussions about racism. The few of them that are willing to talk about it sometimes try to dismiss it as something that is no longer in existence. I believe that the psychology behind this is that many of them feel like racism is such a big problem that it should be avoided, like leprosy. Understandably, many White-presenting people who are aware of the evils their ancestors perpetrated during the slave era are quick to distance themselves from those incidents. For example, in "White Boy" Tom Macdonald, said,

"I cannot feel guilty for shit I didn't do

But I can understand the reasons why you think that I should

Yeah I'm White but I never put your neck in no noose

And I never burnt a cross or hid my face with hood

You can't just label me racist 'cause I'm related to people

Who did some terrible shit way back before I was alive"

Tom is right. No one should hate White-presenting people because they are not all racists. He further explained:

"The White race as a whole ain't the enemy

There are racist White-presenting people but we're far from that collectively

So go ahead and hate the racists, I pray for their extinction

If you wanna hate the White-presenting people, just make a distinction"

I admit that these are beautiful lyrics from a rapper I respect a lot for his creativity, talent, and the desire to spit the truth without any fear of criticism. It would have been easy to accept that whatever happened back then should be forgotten. However, the impacts of those events are still prevalent in the modern world, although in subtle ways.

Inequality Of The Law

One of the pieces of evidence that the impact of racism, as a result of the slave trade era, is still with us today is the inequality of the law. There are instances where two people commit the same crime (one White and one Black) and would receive two different sentences in favor of the White person having a lighter sentence no matter the crime. This reminds me that George Floyd's killer, Derek Chauvine, posted a one million dollar bond and was allowed to roam free for almost one year after killing George Floyd, before receiving his final sentence. Of course, he was eventually prosecuted but the body language wasn't good.

The privileges he enjoyed, even after committing the ultimate crime of taking a human life, are mind-boggling. It questions the credibility of the judicial system in delivering justice for both White-presenting and Visual Minority people. Would a Visual Minority have been allowed to roam that way freely if he had killed a White-presenting person? The prosecution and judgment would have been swift. A situation like this makes it obvious that the lives of some people are worth more than the lives of others, in the US. Both in the case of Emit Till and George Floyd, the body language of the judicial system was questionable.

It feels like the system was very careful and reluctant to prosecute its own for a crime that was committed against an outsider. How are we supposed to agree that the days of the slave trade are far behind us when such incidents still happen in the modern world? These two cases are the exceptional ones that drew the ire of the public but there have been several ones that have gone under the radar.

Dehumanization Through Slavery

To the credit of Tom Macdonald, he said in *White Boy* that his parents raised him to treat people with respect and treat them as equals. In the case of a lovely White-presenting woman I call my friend, she once told me that her grandparents used to tell her that "we always treat our slaves with respect," and that was considered progressive at the time. Indeed, the treatment of slaves wasn't the same during the slave trade era. There was more brutality against slaves in some places, especially the Southern part of the US. They felt such measures were necessary to keep the slaves obedient.

So, if anyone doesn't brutalize his or her slaves, such a person would have been regarded as a "respectful" person back then. Still, the fact that some people felt that others should lose their sense of dignity and freedom in servitude is baffling to me today. How could anyone have looked at another human being and felt that they deserve to be treated like animals because of their skin color? This dehumanization of Visual Minority people for personal gain is still taking its toll even today. It remains the major reason some White-presenting people cannot come to terms with the fact that they should be regarded as equal to Visual Minority people.

Tom is right. White-presenting people should not all be categorized into the same bracket. Indeed, the current sets of people are not the ones that brutalized Visual Minority people during the slave trade era. Still, they have not been able to rectify what their ancestors did. Reparations for the families of people who were slaves have not happened. On the other hand, the families of slave owners still got the money the government of Britain agreed to pay them for losing their "properties" until 2015.

Silent Weapon

Racism was perpetuated through slavery as a "weapon" for keeping Visual Minority people in chains to be in the servitude of the White owners. The era is indeed gone. Yet, that weapon is still active. It has been modernized with modifications that make it capable of having its devastating impact without making the noise it made back in the day. Its current state is worse than the previous one because its activity can easily go unchecked since it is hardly noticed today. It was easy to overcome racism during the slave era because all that needed to be done was to free the slaves.

However, in its current form, it is more challenging to notice it. It has made it easy for some people to even deny its existence. This is why it has been difficult to eradicate racism and why some people feel that it can never go away. Any form of social vice thrives in silence due to the inability of people to identify it. Racism has been so perfectly modified in the modern world, that you could easily think it doesn't exist, especially as a White-presenting person, since you will never have to experience its scourge.

Modern middle-class and bourgeoisie racism are not loud. Racism is mostly silent and subtle in recent times. It is intentionally private and politically correct and, therefore, difficult to notice and understand. It is easily deniable and, in many cases, unconsciously practiced (sometimes intentionally practiced) by many races, and not just White-presenting people. The origin of racism is not taught in history class. Why? It is because the dominant race of White-presenting people historically invented it and did not want to bring attention to it to save face.

Wealth/Education Gap

During the pandemic, many schools in America moved their classes online to facilitate learning without risking the health of the students. Indeed, it was a commendable move, but it was an approach that neglected the wealth/education gap in the US. The people making these decisions are White-presenting people who have enough resources to support their children to sustain that kind of arrangement. Due to the wealth gap in the US, many White-presenting people would be able to provide access to the Internet and devices such as computers that their kids would need for online studies, unlike some Visual Minority families.

It is impossible to separate wealth from education because you will be able to have access to the best available quality of education when you have the resources to finance it. How would people that could barely make ends meet, be able to afford computers and other equipment that would make e-learning possible? Many governmental policies in the US and Canada are made with only White-presenting families in mind without considering the implications for Visual Minority families that don't have what it takes to be able to meet up with what is expected.

The system is built by the White for the White. The hope of Visual Minority people closing the wealth/education gap in the US and Canada is slim as long as things remain the way they are. More White families have the resources that would help them to provide quality education for their children that would increase their chances of getting a good life. On the other hand, many Visual Minority families would have to sacrifice many things to ensure that their children can attend schools and get the level of education that would give them the kind of future they deserve.

Surprise Depositions

White-presenting people's backhanded compliments are intellectually and insultingly unintentional. I taught myself to write the LSAT (a law school entrance exam). I took the test and it taught me all about contra-positives. I observe many White-presenting people being victims of what I call "surprise depositions." This is a situation when you are asked the same questions you ask other people, and they find it inappropriate and insulting to them. The Black Lives Matter movement has prompted many White-presenting people to start asking Visual Minority people questions about racism. However, many of them are emotionally unprepared for what comes after.

Many want us to talk about the future, but they are not ready to talk about the past. How can we have concrete discussions today when we are not willing to start with an honest admission that things have gone wrong before then? B.L Wilson, a correspondent and editor for more than thirty years at NPR, shared her story in *The Washington Post*. According to her, she didn't see her first movie until she was sixteen in 1965. Her grandparents had not allowed her to go to cinemas to see movies before then. She later realized that it was because her grandparents knew that she would not be allowed into the theater before then.

She had thought that her grandparents didn't want her to enjoy her childhood. Unknown to her, they were only trying to protect her from realizing that society regards her as a second-class citizen. In a lunch she had with producers, reporters, and others from mainstream media organizations, most of the people there were White-presenting. She mentioned that she hadn't seen a movie until she was sixteen, to the surprise of most of the people there.

However, once she began to open up the cankerworms of how racial segregation is responsible for the unusual situation, most of the people there began to groan. This is usually the situation. Why are White-presenting people so uncomfortable with discussing issues around racism but want us to forget about the whole thing like it does not exist? Racism is real and it hurts, and more White-presenting people need to realize that.

Bitter Pill Of Reality

I will conclude this chapter by saying some things many White-presenting people hate to hear. Broadly and historically speaking, White-presenting people originally brought about modern-day racism to Canada and the US, and therefore, White-presenting people have the deepest opportunity to fix it. They have the responsibility to lead us away from it by not perpetuating racism through racial education of recent history and racial awareness until the wealth/education gap is closed. It is easy to say but not impossible to achieve since human interactions are always changing. White-presenting people should stop acting as though that era is gone, and its impacts are buried.

Visual Minority people are no longer slaves who have chains in their hands, but many are still incapable of breaking away from the barriers that have been built into the system. Indeed, Visual Minority people are no longer kept in a building like animals that are used on the farm. Yet, the fact remains that Visual Minority people cannot walk around and go wherever they want, without the fear of being profiled by a cop and fined for the most ridiculous reasons. White-presenting people walk around freely, like privileged princes and princesses but Visual Minority people have to sometimes tread carefully to avoid getting into trouble.

As long as most, if not all White-presenting people, are not willing to admit that racism is real and is something they have to take drastic actions about eradicating, we will not make significant progress. Unfortunately, many of them are lackadaisical about the issue and are not even willing to have such conversations because they are not affected. If you are a White-presenting person, you might not have been the one that enslaved Visual Minority people during the slave trade era, but what are you doing to ensure that the impacts of such actions are eradicated in your world and your beliefs? What do you do when or if you notice Visual Minority people being subtly oppressed? Do you criticize the action or keep silent because you are not the victim?

To my White-presenting Sisters and Brothers, in certain cases, your ancestors may indeed have been the ones that perpetrated the evil, but you cannot simply say that you didn't do it. You should want to do all you can to ensure that Visual Minority people are treated with respect today and stand as equals with White-presenting people. Sadly, this is too much of a sacrifice to pay by certain White-presenting people today (as far as they are concerned) because they don't want to lose their social privileges. Many of them love it when they are given opportunities at the expense of Visual Minority people, even when they don't deserve it. So, they are not willing to commit to a cause that can make them lose their undeserved opportunities. This is one of the major reasons racism has been around for so long and it doesn't seem to be going away anytime soon.

Chapter Sixteen:
Uncomfortable Questions For My White-Presenting Brothers And Sisters To Ask Themselves To Continue To Journey Towards Anti-Racism

Learning cannot take place when we are not willing to ask some thought-provoking questions. As a White person that is willing to move from being racially ignorant or racially neutral to being an antiracist, there are some questions you need to ask yourself and answer. Many of such questions will be highlighted in this chapter.

When was the last time I had an anti-racist dialogue with a fellow White person?

This is a crucial question that will help you to know your disposition towards racism. If it has never happened before, it might mean that you are racially ignorant. If it only happens once in a while, it might mean that you are racially neutral. However, if it happens consistently whenever you have the opportunity, it is a sign that you are racially active. It shows that you are concerned about the pains and the struggles of Visual Minority people and you are willing to do something about it. If you have not been having these kinds of conversations before now, you should start considering it. Try to initiate them whenever possible because White-presenting people would be less apprehensive and defensive to talk about racism when speaking to another White-presenting person.

How can I use my White privilege to help others?

You should use your privileges in life to help those that are not as privileged as you are. If you are a rich person, you should be aware that many people around you cannot make ends meet. Indeed, you don't owe them anything, but it is always a good and commendable act when you choose to reach out to them to help them. In the same way, you can use your White privilege to be the voice of the voiceless. There are social media platforms where you can speak intelligently and sincerely as a White-presenting person and you would be taken more seriously than when a Visual Minority speaks. Take advantage of these platforms to make White supremacists consider reforms that will bring about racial equality and eliminate segregation.

Am I aware, or afraid, or unwilling to feel 'White guilt' for having White privilege and entitlement?

Guilt is not a positive emotion and that is why nobody wants to experience it. Still, you need to experience it sometimes as a human being. When you feel guilty for something that is not right, it shows that you have human feelings and empathy. As a White person, if you experience guilt for the fact that years of segregation and racial discrimination have given you White privilege and entitlement, it is a good thing. It is a feeling that will inspire you to try to right the wrongs. On the other hand, if you don't care that you have undue advantages over others, it is a sign that you need to revamp your value system as soon as possible.

Do I tend to take the professional or expert advice of White-presenting people more seriously than professional or expert advice of Visual Minority people?

We all want to get the best possible services from professionals because suggestions and recommendations have consequences. Still, you can check your disposition to racism based on how you consider the expert advice given by a White person compared to when it is given by a Visual Minority. If you tend to take what a White professional says more seriously than what a Visual Minority expert says, it is a sign that you still have elements of racial discrimination in your heart that you need to resolve as soon as possible. Anybody can be fake or a quack regardless of their race. In another way, expertise, professional training, and expert education have nothing to do with skin color. You need to convince yourself about this fact and you will find out that it is ubiquitously true, and also true in the long run.

If I were sick, would I feel more comfortable with a White doctor treating my children, or a Visual Minority doctor treating my children?

This question is similar to the last question. However, this is more vital because it has to do with what concerns us all the most – our health, specifically the health of our children. Your children's health is not something you can toy with because their life depends on it. So, it is understandable to be very careful before you can trust anyone in this area. Still, you have to trust doctors because they have been trained, and they have the expertise that is required to help in this regard. If you feel more comfortable when you and your children are treated by a White-presenting doctor than when a Visual Minority doctor is in charge, it is a sign that you have to do something about your racial values.

If I were to hire a pilot to fly me across the ocean, what would make me feel the safest, a White-presenting pilot or a Visual Minority pilot?

This is another tricky question that scrutinizes whether you trust people. It is a question that can easily help you to know whether you trust people based on their race or their qualifications. When flying an airplane over the ocean, you are trusting the pilot with your life because you know that nothing must go wrong. So, it is natural that you would want to ensure that a trained person, that has what it takes to do a good job, is in charge. If you feel that a White-presenting person would do a better job than a Visual Minority, it is a sign that you have racial biases. It shouldn't matter whether the pilot is a male, female, Visual Minority, or White-presenting. What should matter to you is whether the person is qualified to do the job or not, and that has nothing to do with gender or race.

Looking back over the years, has my Whiteness contributed to my success and self-confidence in some way? How?

We all want to be successful in life and self-confidence is crucial in that regard. Without self-confidence, you will have low self-esteem. You need confidence in your ability to carry out a task before you embark on it. When you are confident, there are certain things you consider that give you that feeling. It could be because you have worked hard and done the necessary assignments that will give you a higher chance to succeed. If your confidence to succeed comes from the fact that you are White, it is a bad omen. It is a sign that you feel that you are superior to people from minority races. When you have this mindset, you will never want to be a part of any reform that can lead to racial equality.

Has the color of my skin ever held me back from achieving anything in any way?

The answer to this question will be "no" for most White-presenting people. The only way you can be affected by the color of your skin as a White-presenting person is if you meet a person from a minority race that is deliberately trying to deny you what you deserve as a form of revenge for all the atrocities of White-presenting people against Visual Minority people. In a regular situation, no one would judge you wrongly by denying you the opportunities you deserve as a White-presenting person. On the other hand, Visual Minority people experience this so many times. This is one of the reasons you should want to be a part of the struggle against racism to ensure that others don't lose the opportunities they deserve because of their race.

What would it be like to live your life over again if you weren't White-presenting? And would you want to?

You need to consider this question so that you can be concerned about how people from other races are treated. What if you were not White-presenting? How would you feel if people treated you wrongly and judged you with different standards because of your skin color? This is exactly what happens to Visual Minority people almost daily. If you cannot imagine being a Visual Minority because of the White entitlement and privilege you would lose, then you should leverage your position to cause a change in society. Empathy is the ability to put yourself in the shoes of others. If being a Visual Minority would mean that you would face racial discrimination, then you should be committed to putting an end to it.

Why is it that I know so little or nothing about Black slavery? Why didn't my school system go into depth to teach me about Black slavery, or in a way that inspired empathy for my fellow human beings?

These are the questions that make Visual Minority people question the intention of the people at the helm of affairs. Why are they historically and currently not allowing White-presenting people to fully know about this part of our history? The obvious answer would have been that it is because they are not proud of what happened in the past. It is okay to be disappointed about what happened in the past, but it is a problem when we are not committed to correcting the ills of those events. The presence of systemic racial discrimination in the modern world is proof that White children are not exposed to Black slavery history, to prevent them from questioning the system and pulling it down.

When was the last time I had a Visual Minority over for dinner in my home?

If you have Visual Minority people come over to your home for dinner, it is a sign that you don't see them as inferior individuals to your race. However, if you have never had them come to your home for dinner before, it could be a sign that you don't have any form of professional or interpersonal relationship with Visual Minority people. If this is the case, does it not bother you? If you have Visual Minority colleagues or neighbors, naturally and over time, you should try to invite them over for dinner once in a while because this will help you to know and understand them better, but don't force it.

Do I have any Visual Minority friends?

If you don't have Visual Minority friends, what could be responsible for that? Is it because you didn't find any or have you been too careful to ensure that you don't have Visual Minority people as friends? If you are not open to being a friend to a Visual Minority, why is that the case? Is it because of an experience you have had before with people from another race that is not pleasant? Friendship is what helps people to discover who they are and learn about their culture. So, if you intend to open yourself to a different culture and know them, you should want to have Visual Minority people as your friends. Note, social privilege can make it easier for a White-presenting person to start a friendship with a Visual Minority than when the onus is on the Visual Minority.

Have I ever had a Visual Minority friend before?

It is possible that you no longer have a BIPOC friend now due to many reasons. It could be that the friend you used to have had traveled elsewhere and the relationship is no longer what it used to be due to distance. Still, have you ever had one before? If your answer to that question is "no" then you can never have an objective basis for judging Visual Minority people. You will only feed on assumptions, which might not be true. So, it is best for your experience as a human being to explore starting a friendship with people from other races. This will help you to have such people close enough to you to make objective conclusions about their way of life and who they are.

Have I ever confided in, or deeply trusted, a Visual Minority as a confidante?

Whenever you are willing to share the things that matter to you with another person, it is a sign that you trust the person. You act that way when you believe that the person will not use the information against you. If you have Visual Minority people that you trust enough to share the things that matter to you, it is a sign that you are a White Visual Minority person that doesn't have issues with relating to people of color. On the other hand, if you have never had anyone like that and can hardly imagine it happening, it shows that you have work to do. Of course, you cannot just trust people just because you don't want to appear racist. You should start with a friendship that you will build over time.

Why aren't there more Visual Minority people living in my neighborhood? Would I want more Visual Minority people living in my neighborhood? How would living with more Visual Minority people in my neighborhood make me feel?

No one wants to live in a neighborhood that is hostile to his or her race. So, you should wonder why Visual Minority people are not living in your neighborhood if that is the case. You should not see it as a normal thing when you don't have people from other races living where you live. It could be a sign that your neighborhood is hostile to them. If it is a relatively expensive neighborhood, it could be a sign that the wealth and education gap in our society has made it almost impossible for Visual Minority people to be able to afford to live in that kind of place. You should also ask yourself if you would be comfortable living with Visual Minority people in your neighborhood. If you are not, your attitude could be a carbon copy of the perception of the people that live around the place.

Have I ever been curious about Visual Minority culture before? If not, why?

Curiosity is a crucial part of learning. It is curiosity that will make you ask the necessary questions that will help you to understand an idea or concept. You should not make assumptions about anything because they might be wrong. It is always better to make proper findings before you conclude. If you have never been curious about Visual Minority culture, it is not a good sign. It reveals that you are not interested in understanding them and knowing how they are different or the same as you. Every human culture overlaps in certain aspects. For example, every human culture teaches respect, but the way they go about it varies. If you have not been curious about Visual Minority culture, you should work towards it.

Am I a part of the problem of racism, or am I part of the solution to racism?

This question is tricky but simple when you are not biased. Some people think that they automatically are not part of a problem when they are not involved in creating it. It is not always true, especially in the case of racism. One of the reasons racism continues to thrive in the modern world is that many White-presenting people are enjoying White privilege and entitlement in silence. If you are not doing anything to help to achieve racial equity, you are automatically part of the problem. It means that you are one of the White-presenting people that are enjoying the inequalities that years of enslaving Visual Minority people had accomplished in our society. So, if you don't want to be a part of the problem, you need to start being deliberate about helping to end this evil.

What are the self-respecting moral consequences of NOT becoming a more engaging part of the solution to racism? And what kind of example would I be

leaving behind knowing what I know about the nature and mechanisms of racism?

Life becomes more worthwhile when we are part of something that transcends us. It is mundane and sedentary to be comfortable with just making money and having fun. Life is worth more than that. We are here at such a time as this to be a part of the solutions to the problems in our society. Racism is one of those problems that have to be solved as soon as possible. You cannot be happy with yourself if the battle against racism is eventually won without your input. You will be disappointed in yourself because you know that you could have done something but ultimately did nothing. You have the chance to avoid living with that regret by being deliberate about being a part of the solution to racism. Don't throw the opportunity to be part of the solution to racism away.

Have I been unintentionally ignoring racial integration?

Racial integration is the responsibility of us all, especially White-presenting people. The simple reason White-presenting people have more responsibility is that they are the ones that historically started racism in Canada and the US and they are the beneficiaries of the legacies of racial segregation. So, they must be more open to seeing Visual Minority people as equals and extend a hand of friendship to them. If you have not been actively involved in this, you have been unintentionally ignoring racial integration. You still have time to turn this around by seeking opportunities to create platforms that will enable you to be able to have productive conversations with Visual Minority people. Naturally, Visual Minority people wouldn't want to be the first to initiate a conversation with a White person. Let them know that you will not snub them and are willing to talk to them intelligently.

In honestly answering these questions, what have I learned about myself? And are there any perceptions (no matter how small) I've discovered that need to change? If so, what are they? And what can I do to inspire racial awareness in others, and peacefully lead by example in my circle of friends and family?

This is the final array of questions to seriously consider. It is what will help you to move from being racially ignorant or racially neutral to being an antiracist. Remember that when it comes to the issue of racism, you cannot sit on the fence. A Visual Minority that is not doing anything about racism will not be contributing to the solution but is not making it worse. Such a person has simply chosen to suffer in silence. However, if a White-presenting person is not willing to be a part of the solution to racism, he or she may be unintentionally contributing to the problem. I am not trying to guilt-trip you. I am simply urging and encouraging you to start contributing your quota to end racism because the solutions need us all to roll up our sleeves and engage in any way we can.

Chapter Seventeen: Uncomfortable Questions For My Visual Minority Brothers And Sisters To Ask Themselves To Begin To Process The Effects Of Living With Inequality

In this chapter, we will explore certain uncomfortable questions for Visual Minority people. These questions will help you to know where you are and what you can do to ensure that you overcome racism.

Has racism left me feeling battle fatigued?

Naturally, you feel this way sometimes because the battle against racism has been going on for some time and it doesn't seem like it is coming to an end any time soon. Meanwhile, the pain that comes with facing this reality goes on every day. You still have to strive against the barriers built into the system to prevent you from enjoying the same opportunities and privileges available to White-presenting people. The feeling is overwhelming, and you might just feel like giving up. I also feel that way sometimes but giving up is not an option. If you did give up, what would happen to the effort of all the people that have lost their lives in this struggle? What would it mean?

The least we owe them is to refuse to give up. It might not look as though we have made significant progress in recent times. Still, the fact is that we are no longer where we used to be. I admit that the progress has been slow but at least we are not working backward. If we give up, who else will stand for us? We are the victims of this evil and we must continue to stand strong until our dream comes true. This battle is greater than us. It is more than what we stand to benefit from now. Rather, the future of our children also depends on it. So, we cannot afford to fail them by giving up now.

How well can I tell the difference between an ignorantly racist White-presenting person and an anti-racist White-presenting person? And could I stand to improve my perceptions of the two?

You must tell the difference between the two so that you can know who to avoid and who to keep around you. Of course, you should not assume anything about people and you shouldn't believe that a racially ignorant person cannot improve. A racially ignorant person is a product of a lack of exposure to the culture of other people and you should be willing to help such people. Naturally, you would be angry when a person doesn't show you equal respect. You would be put off and would feel like retaliating and showing the person that you are not a pushover. Still, if you are patient, you might end up winning the person over.

Always be willing to give people opportunities to grow and repent. This is one of the ways we can help racially ignorant people. When you are patient with them when they use words that are socially and racially unacceptable, there's always a chance that they might be willing to listen to you, get enlightened, and correct their ways. No one is an expert when it comes to knowing the difference between a racially ignorant person and an anti-racist, because the difference can be extremely subtle sometimes. You will get better in your ability to distinguish between them over time, based on learning from your experiences and paying attention to the rational and wise sides of your instincts.

On the subject of inequality, what do I do with my spirited feelings, and how can I process them peacefully?

Naturally, you are angry when you study the history of racism. The more I discovered the atrocities committed against our ancestors by the Colonial White-presenting people, the angrier I got. I couldn't imagine why a generation could have been full of wicked people that enslaved fellow human beings and treated them like animals and worse. The dehumanization stirs up negative emotions and makes me want to dislike certain White-presenting people. So, you are not alone if you feel that way. Still, you must process your feelings peacefully. This is necessary for your mental health and it will also help you not to be stirred up to do something you might regret.

You cannot afford to allow yourself to be overwhelmed by anger in such a way that it makes you want to hurt White-presenting people. So, instead of just getting angry and all of that, let your disappointment become positive energy that will be used to overcome racism. Let your disappointment make you determined to do all you can to end racism in our society. I know that converting negative emotions into positive energy is easier said than done, but you have to do it for the sake of your mental health, and for the sake of making the world a better place.

As I learn more about the historic perspectives of racism, how can I forgive humanity's ancestral atrocities to give their descendants a chance at dialogue that my ancestors should have had?

Forgiveness is crucial in helping us to let go of past hurts and to create platforms for building relationships. We have to share this world with White-presenting people whether we like it or not. We need them and they also need us. So, disliking them will not lead us anywhere. The reality is that most, if not all the people that did those evil things to our ancestors, are no longer alive. Even if they were alive, we would not gain anything from hating them. What we should seek is reconciliation. Of course, it helps when the other party admits its wrongs, apologizes, and is willing to act better.

Yet even when that is not happening, we must be willing to forgive because that is the only way we can give the other person the opportunity to eventually come around to make things right. We should see the situation like a former neighbor that treated us wrongly. You will have to forgive him for your mental health because carrying pain hurts, and long-standing pain is not good for you. Still, that doesn't mean that you shouldn't hold him or her accountable for his or her actions. Stating the facts doesn't mean that you are angry. We will continue to state the facts so that White-presenting people can understand what has happened and how they can make amends. Still, we have to forgive them for our own sake.

How can I peacefully articulate the nuances of inequity when oppression presents itself to me, without feeling like I have to ignore my feelings to blend in?

Suffering in silence is never a good thing because you will keep getting hurt without expressing it. In some cases, the person hurting you might not realize it because you are not saying anything. You cannot ignore your feelings because they are real. The fact that White-presenting people get apprehensive, uncomfortable, and defensive doesn't mean that we should stop conversations about racial discrimination and segregation. Still, we have to go about it in a way that is devoid of rage and other negative emotions. It is normal and healthy to be passionate about defending your race but you shouldn't allow anger to get the better of you.

When the opponent notices that you are angry and resentful, they will use it against you. Therefore, you must keep your cool while articulating your opinion. If you notice that you are getting angry, take a few deep breaths and relax. Speak with passion but don't let rage creep into your countenance. Be firm and straight to the point. State the facts and make your points clear. Let anyone who cares to listen know that racism is a disease that should be cured as soon as possible. Give the opponents reason to have a rethink but never allow them to have reasons to accuse you based on your approach.

How can I trust an anti-racist White-presenting person enough to share my perspectives and stories without expecting judgment or condescending minimization in return?

You just have to go for it. Like I said in the last answer, ensure that you present your points without allowing anger to creep into the conversation. Remember that an anti-racist White-presenting person has emotions and he or she still has the tendency to defend his or her race. So, be careful to avoid pushing them to a point when they will be forced to be defensive. When talking about White ancestors to an anti-racist White-presenting person, ensure that you attack the wrong actions and not the people. You cannot afford to say such things as "White-presenting people are so evil and terrible."

The person might feel insulted when you talk like that and might be put off by the way you speak. So, learn to state the facts without attacking the White race. Don't allow the sentiments of the person to get the better of him or her because of your approach to the discussion. This is the only way you can get the attention of the person without making him or her want to be defensive in any way. Always give anyone that comes to you as a White-presenting anti-racist, the benefit of the doubt. If they detect that you have doubts about them from the onset, it might make them lose interest in the conversation. Don't let your attitude ruin the opportunities for intelligent and sincere dialogue.

How can I allow myself enough mental and emotional rest from the stress of navigating, or preparing to navigate, living in a Visual Majority world as a Visual Minority?

Indeed, it is not every time that you will be in the mood to want to answer racially related questions. The battle against racism is mentally draining because it hurts when others treat you with disdain and disrespect because of your race. Like I said earlier, your race is not something you can change. No amount of bleaching can change the fact that you are a Visual Minority. So, at different points, you will have to battle the barriers that have been built into the system to prevent you from getting the opportunities you deserve. Every single time, it will hurt again, and the aggravation may return. Still, you have to learn to give yourself a mental break sometimes.

This doesn't mean that you should be lackadaisical about the issue. You cannot afford to cross to that other side. Yet, you shouldn't let the issue overwhelm you. The barriers are there, and we have no idea when they will be removed. So, I encourage you to try to make the best of the situation in the meantime. We will not stop pushing to get what we deserve. Still, you have to live your life as much as possible. Keep training yourself and keep adding value to yourself. Even amid racial segregation, you have to be prepared so that you will be able to take advantage of the opportunities that come your way.

Chapter Eighteen:
Consequences For Not Exposing Yourself To New Cultures And Consequences For Avoiding Multicultural Dialogue With Those Outside Of Your Culture

In Obama's response to how to solve racism in America, he spoke about being willing to expose yourself to other cultures. He emphasized the importance of being willing to know people that are not like us. This is a crucial step toward eradicating racism from our society. If we don't do this, there are consequences to it. In this chapter, we will explore the things that can go wrong when we try to maintain a "safe distance" from people that don't belong to our race.

Wrong Assumptions About The White Race

Thinking that taking a racial neutrality position is good enough when, in fact, it isn't is one of the reasons things haven't improved yet in America and Canada. Some people have this funny idea that time will sort things out. There are indeed some things that will become clearer over time that will make us make better decisions. However, the reality is that time doesn't solve problems by itself. Rather, it is our input over time that will determine the kind of results we will get eventually. For example, if Emit Till's mother didn't take the radical action she took when her son was murdered, we might not have been able to achieve Civil Rights.

Problems are never solved if we just leave them to time. We must be willing to make commitments and be ready to be a part of the solution. Racism has been around for so long because many of us are not deliberate about solving this problem. Being neutral isn't good enough. If you are a White person, not being racist is not enough. In the same way, if you are a person of color, accepting the impacts of racism will only ensure that we and the future generation will continue to suffer from the various barriers set up against us due to segregation and racial discrimination.

If a barrier is in your living room that keeps making it difficult for you to navigate around the room, you cannot leave it there and hope that something will happen that will take the barrier away. You will have to create time to find a way to remove it so that you can have more space. For White-presenting folks, the fact that you are not affected shouldn't make you keep quiet. If you are silent, things will continue to get worse for Visual Minority people. How is that supposed to be your problem, right? I will attempt to help you with that.

If Visual Minority people keep getting suppressed and discriminated against, it can lead to them hating White-presenting people and targeting them for attacks to retaliate for their sufferings. I know it sounds crazy, and it is not a good situation, but things can get that bad if we don't all rise up to solve this problem. How will anyone know what you think about racism when you don't speak up? When you notice a criminal entering your neighbor's house to steal his goods and you say nothing, it would be assumed that you connived with the criminal. In the same way, when you see the suffering of Visual Minority people due to racism and you are silent, it is assumed that you approve of it.

The Problem Will Be Prolonged

Even before the days of Martin Luther King, the struggle for racial equality has been on. He lost his life in the struggle, but it has not ended. If we continue to display apathy towards racism, the sacrifices of people like Martin Luther King would be a waste because the problem will remain unresolved. Visual Minority people protesting and complaining will never be enough to solve the problem. We need more White-presenting people that will be willing to contribute their efforts to help restore sanity to our society. It took the collaborative efforts of Visual Minority and White-presenting people to help Visual Minority slaves to escape from their captivity in the American South to the American North during the slave era.

This is the kind of attitude and energy we need to continue to press towards the finish line today. A crucial part of achieving victory against racism is to have more White-presenting people that are willing to **deliberately** take steps to know people that are not from their race.

Forget about what your parents told you or what you saw in the media. Be open to new experiences. This doesn't mean that you should throw caution to the wind, as I often reiterate. Still, you should be willing to talk to Visual Minority people without any ulterior motive as a White-presenting person.

Try to understand the way they think and their struggles without any form of assumption. This problem has been around for too long and we need to bring it to an end. Don't you want to live in a world where people are not afraid of being invisibly oppressed because of their skin color? I want to be a part of that world. I want to be able to stay around White-presenting people without feeling any form of inferiority. I want to be able to have White-presenting colleagues that I have productive conversations with, without feeling that they secretly dismiss me or resent me.

As a White-presenting person, I am convinced that you also want to be a part of that America and Canada where you are not afraid that someone hates your kids and families because of the undue privileges they have. Tom Macdonald highlighted this fear in *White Boy* when he said:

"I got a mother, a father, a sister, an auntie, an uncle, and a grandma that I picture when you're openly hatin.' And God willing one day, I'll have a kid of my own. I refuse to let you blindly hate my wife or baby."

Tom is right about the fact that Visual Minority people shouldn't hate White-presenting people because of the assumption that they are all racists. However, the reality is that some Visual Minority people may have this notion if things continue this way. Racism is the common enemy, and we need to uproot it to avoid pain on both sides.

Lack Of Execution Of Plans

We can go ahead to create excellent strategies that will enable us to curb racism, but nothing will be achieved until White-presenting people start doing their part. Racism is not an act that is perpetrated by faceless people. Historically, it is White-presenting people that have created a system that is making life difficult for Visual Minority people. Permit me to quote Tom Macdonald again in *White Boy*:

"If you wanna hate the White-presenting people, just make a distinction between the ones who want the best for everyone regardless and the ones who built the system just to smother you with hardship."

Tom was trying to tell Visual Minority people to make a distinction when hating White-presenting people here. Still, he also admitted that it is White-presenting people that built the system to smother Visual Minority people with hardship. This is a vital fact that every White-presenting person must admit. If White-presenting people built the system to make life difficult for Visual Minority people, then the good White-presenting people that Tom said "want the best for everyone regardless" need to stand up for Visual Minority people. We have been at this same spot for years because many White-presenting people are enjoying the way the system is built.

You cannot claim that you are not a racist when you are not willing to speak up against a racist system just because it profits you. Dear Tom, we need these good White-presenting people to start speaking up more so that we can identify them and channel our energy in the right direction. We need them to start being deliberate in their resolve to end racism by interacting more with Visual Minority people. They should be more willing to have open and honest conversations about racism. Their silence has been deafening and it is high time that changed.

Saying that you were not the ones that bought, sold, and mistreated Visual Minority slaves is no longer good enough. It is when you take conscious steps to disassemble the system to give Visual Minority people the same opportunities that are available to White-presenting people that you can be taken seriously. Enough of sitting on the fence and claiming that you didn't build the system. If you don't approve of this racist system, then consider taking concrete actions to pull it down.

The least you can do is to be open to reaching out to Visual Minority people and try to understand their pain. Be open to their culture and experience so that you can see things from their point of view. Dear modern-day White-presenting brother or sister, we cannot believe that you are not a racist just because you say that you are not. We know that you didn't build the system, but we need your help to level the playing field.

Continuous Disparity In The Human Race

We have indeed done so much as human beings to make the world a better place. We have invented so many machines to make life better among several discoveries. Still, I am convinced that we are yet to harness our full potential as human beings because of segregation and racism. The education gap between White-presenting and Visual Minority people in Developed Countries, guarantees that we will keep losing great talent that could have performed great exploits to make the world a better place. We need all human beings to make their contributions to give us a better world.

Sidelining some people by building a system that favors one race over the other will continue to limit us. During the US civil war, the Union Army could have failed if it didn't allow Visual Minority people to contribute their efforts during the war. Many of them served with distinction during the war and got national recognition. This and many more are what can happen when we eliminate racism and allow everybody to fulfill their potential. If those Visual Minority people were not allowed to show what they could do by enlisting them and empowering them, they could not have displayed the heroics they showed.

We live in a world today where we are careful because we don't want to get hurt. One of the reasons this is happening to us is racial segregation. If Visual Minority and White-presenting people could interact freely and have meaningful racial conversations, we will be able to build a society where we care more for one another. When you are not willing to expose yourself to the culture of others, you will miss out on experiencing feelings of connection and belonging you aren't aware of and have yet to fully engage. It is always a beautiful thing to experience the culture of others without any form of misgiving.

You don't have to believe or accept every practice that a set of people possess. Yet, when you consider the values of people from an objective point of view, you would be able to understand why they see things that way and you might even be able to help them to see it in a better way. Many of the Christian missionaries that went to Africa were able to improve the lives of the people because they were willing to expose themselves to the people's culture. Their openness made the people willing to accept certain areas of their beliefs that needed to be modified to improve the quality of their lives.

Risk Of Continuous Hatred

When you don't take action that can help us to solve this problem of racism, you run the risk of passing on the disease to the next generation instead of helping to cure it for them. We should all want to derive pleasure from the fact that we were part of the people that brought an end to a social ill in our generation. The generation that did all they could until Civil Rights became a reality in America would have been very proud of what they achieved with their effort. Our lives become worthless when it is not used to serve a purpose that is greater than us.

This problem has been with us for too long, and we have the opportunity to bring an end to it if only we are willing to do the needful. Come to think of it, you would be proud if you had the opportunity to tell your grandchildren about the role you played to eradicate racism from your society towards the end of your life. If racism is eventually eradicated and you didn't play an active role, you would have nothing to say when people talk about the individuals that helped in ending the problem. We should not be content with just making money and climbing up to the top of the ladder in our careers.

We should also be interested in making changes in our society that will be to the benefit of generations to come. It will be disappointing if the next generation has to battle racism because we did nothing about it while we were here. The reality is that racism is a problem. Therefore, any generation will suffer from its impact and legacy. What if the next generation thought, "The older generation failed us by their inability to eradicate this issue before we were born, even though some of them fought hard and did all that they could."

This is our opportunity to right the wrongs. Older White-presenting generations began racism and built the system that favors White-presenting people above Visual Minority people. Yet, the younger generation of White-presenting people has maintained the status quo. Many of them claim that they would never have treated Visual

Minority people the way their ancestors did but the fact that they have not done anything significant to eradicate racism remains, maintaining a figurative whip that could be used to lash others. If you want to be taken seriously, you need to move from being racially neutral to being an antiracist. Engage in more conversations with Visual Minority people and try to have a better understanding of their culture by fostering genuine cultural curiosity about Minorities.

Feeding Ignorance While Squashing Wisdom At The Same Time

In that classic Obama response, he said that we need to let our children understand that the legacies of racism, such as the wealth gap, arrest rate, and incarceration, didn't just appear out of the blue. This is a crucial thing that is missing today. Many Americans and Canadians are not aware of how we got to this point. Many assume that Visual Minority people are discriminated against because they are bad and unproductive people. Many of them are not aware that we got here because of years of Black slavery by White slave masters.

Schools barely teach White-presenting children this dirty part of our history because they are trying to save face. However, we cannot just act as though those terrible things never happened simply because we live in another generation. The impacts of those things are still here, and we are not making significant progress to eradicate them. When you are not willing to open yourself to experience a new culture as a White-presenting person, we will continue in this redundant circle where ignorance continues to reign about racism and what brought it about. Our children and the current generations need to be enlightened about what happened to our ancestors so that they can be more encouraged to right their wrongs.

Doing nothing does not show that you are not a racist. Rather, it shows that you enjoy White privileges and entitlements that are conferred on you as a result of the legacies of the slave trade era. Being neutral and sitting in your comfort zone does not speak well of you as a White person. If for instance, my father was a corrupt politician and I am attending the best schools from the proceeds of his crimes and extortion, I might be ashamed or at least embarrassed. In that case, keeping quiet and spending the money would only show that I am glad that my father did all the things he did to give me the kind of life I have.

Alienation From The Human Race

Your experiences and references in life are not complete when you have no idea how other people live and how they go about their lives. If you don't decide to navigate a path from a position of racial indifference to a position of anti-racism, you will always be more separate from the human race than you realize. Like Obama said in his response to racism, you cannot understand other people when you only speak to the people that are like you and laugh at the jokes that are funny to you. This is one of the key reasons many White-presenting people are racially ignorant.

Many of them have been cracking jokes that mock Visual Minority people with other White-presenting people and it was perfectly okay. They have never had someone correct them that their actions are inappropriate. So, they are surprised at the backlash they receive when they say the same things in public places. Such people are living in a cocoon. They have a limited and myopic view of the world. They don't have all-around experiences of other cultures to know when they are out of bounds. You don't have to be embarrassed publicly before you realize that some words are racially inappropriate.

Bernando Silva, a Portuguese football player for Manchester City in England, was fined for such conduct towards Benjamin Mendy, his teammate. He used a racially inappropriate word to refer to Mendy (I'll let you speculate what this word was), who is a Visual Minority French player. He claimed to be joking and his coach, Pep Guardiola, also defended him. However, the authorities made him a scapegoat. Maybe Silva didn't mean to hurt Mendy by speaking to him that way. He might just be racially ignorant. Still, you don't joke with sensitive words. Silva learned the hard way. This is what can happen to you when you don't have enough exposure to the culture of other people to know what is deemed appropriate and what is acceptable to them.

Multicultural Dialogue All The Way

This final point is not one of the problems you can encounter when you don't expose yourself to the culture of other people. Rather, it is an emphasis on a crucial way we can resolve racism in this generation.

Racism is a disease attacking the soul of humanity, and humanity's unrealized multicultural dialogue is the path to a cure. Remember, our words when we dialogue can either heal or they can hurt. So, use your words wisely. You can ruin a friendship of many years by saying the wrong things in a way that can lead to irreconcilable differences.

In the same way, you can ruin your marriage when you inappropriately speak to your spouse. Words are powerful and should never be used without consequential thinking. This same principle applies when dealing with racism. We can speak to people from other cultures in a way that they will feel appreciated and respected. On the other hand, you can talk to people from other races in a way that will make them start avoiding you or, worse still, attack you.

The way you sincerely talk to people is an investment that will yield dividends. If you show respect and affection, you will reap the same. You can reap them one hundredfold. On the other hand, when you show disrespect and dishonor, be ready to reap the consequences a thousandfold. Our society is crying for mutual respect and love. We have the opportunity to be that generation that turned this around. Let's get to work and interact more. Let's break cultural barriers and make defrauded policies whole.

Chapter Nineteen:
Solutions To Racism

We have spent most parts of this book talking about the problem of racism and its devastating impact. It is befitting that in this last section we begin to explore some of the possible solutions. The truth is that there is no single solution to this problem. Still, some can be considered.

The Path To Anti-Racism

Although many books have been written and several studies have shown that regular exercise has multiple health benefits, there are still many people that are not involved in regular exercise. What could be responsible for this? It is because exercise can be painful and stressful – more for some than for others. This illustrates the reason many people are not ready to be involved in the struggle against racism. It is full of emotional turmoil. As a Visual Minority, you are used to the pain already. You see it every day and you have to live through it.

However, as a White-presenting person, if you are willing to help out and be a part of the change our society craves, you must first be willing to try to understand the pain and the emotional disturbances that come with being treated differently because of your race. You don't have to be a woman to demand the rights of women. You only need to understand the pain that comes with being treated like a weakling and an insignificant person, all because you are a woman before you can demand their rights and defend them.

In the same way, you don't have to be a Visual Minority to be able to defend the rights of Visual Minority people. What you need to do is to first begin with trying to understand the pains of Visual Minority people. Note that the pains and emotional disturbances travel as far back as the slave trade era. You cannot claim that you care about a person and not be interested in their family. If you hold a person in high esteem, you must be willing to accept the pains of the person's loved ones too. Take your time to study the history of racism and know for yourself and on your own how we got here.

When you travel backward, you will be able to help yourself understand what happened and how you can deal with it today. Visual Minority people are put off by White-presenting people who try to show interest in discussing racism but are not willing to hear everything about it. Don't expect a person that has been a victim of segregation to be calm when talking about it. He might show signs of annoyance and other deep-seated resentments. You must be willing to understand all of that to have honest conversations. That's called real talk.

Eliminating The Lack Of Inconsequential Thinking

One of the ways racism can be eliminated is by addressing the lack of inconsequential thinking among White-presenting people that are involved in racist actions. You can never display empathy when you lack consequential thinking. Consequential thinking is reasoning about how your actions can affect a person before you carry them out. As human beings, we are different from animals because we are rational. We can train ourselves perfectly to be less impulsive. In other words, we don't act just because we feel like it. Animals are impulsive. They can have sex anywhere once they feel like it, regardless of who is looking at them.

They don't have any sense of shame. Human beings are not supposed to act that way. A human being is supposed to think about what might happen when he or she does something. Words and actions are powerful. They can be as powerful as missiles. Once you release them, you will never be able to stop their impact. You cannot just believe that you would apologize for whatever you do and whatever you say. There are some things you do that no amount of apologies would be able to make up for. When you racially abuse a person, you might apologize for the offense, but the damage has been done already.

When someone else says something similar to the person at another time and place, the person would remember what you said earlier, and the wound would be opened again. So, it is better that you don't do the wrong things at all rather than think that an apology would be enough to make up for what you have done. In this case, you should be sensitive about how your words can affect Visual Minority people when you make jokes about their ancestry or make mocking remarks related to their skin color.

It is when you understand the pain that your words and actions can cause, that you would be more careful about what you say and do to others. So, you must begin by understanding how Visual Minority people feel when you speak racially derogatory words to them or deny them the opportunities they deserve because of their skin color. It is better to avoid such words and actions because of how they can hurt others. This is what empathy is all about.

How Can White-presenting People Talk To Visual Minority People?

It is simply a respectful mindset. Every relationship is based on the understanding of the likes and dislikes of the other person. You cannot have a functional relationship with a person when you are not willing to understand the things the person likes and the things that hurt the person. In the uncomfortable racial conversations with Visual Minority people, White-presenting people must be sensitive, to avoid saying things that can bring back the hurt of racism and the anguish of the slave era. This doesn't mean that a White-presenting person cannot be free around a Visual Minority. It is simply being aware of the things that mean a lot to another person and also being conscious of the things that can cause pain to him or her.

Being willing to accept that your actions can hurt another person is a simple and strong sign of respect. It shows that you care about how the person feels. It is the basic expectation in every relationship. No one wants to be around a person that doesn't respect him or her. If I come around to you and you have a culture of disregarding the things I value, I will see you as an insensitive person that should be avoided. No matter how close you are to a person, there are some things you should never joke about. It is not true that you can say whatever you want to a person just because they are your friend.

Friendship should come with mutual respect. A person shouldn't have to put up with your insensitive words. The people around you shouldn't wish that they never met you. You might not have a Visual Minority as your friend, but you might have them as your colleagues, neighbors, or fitness group partner. Regardless of the nature of the relationship, you should be sensitive to their feelings. Of course, this should be mutual. The people in your life should also be aware of the things they might do that can affect your emotions.

Anyone that is not willing to treat you with respect should not be in your life. You should avoid them as much as possible because they will only make you experience negative emotions. So, as a White-presenting person, the key to your interaction and relationship with people from other races is to be aware of where to draw the line. If you have a lady who had been raped before as your friend, you have to be careful when you talk about rape around her. In the same way, when you have Visual Minority people around you, you should be aware that racial slurs and slang will get to them.

President Obama's Thoughts

The first Visual Minority president of the US, Barack Obama, weighed in on what he thinks the probable solutions to racism are when he was asked by YouTuber Emmanuel Acho. He began by brilliantly reminding us all that there is no silver bullet solution to this problem. He also said that people discriminate against people they feel are outsiders. Still, in the American context, he said he believes three things can help. According to him, the first one is:

"Making sure that our kids know our history, right? That the inequalities we have today do exist, whether it's in terms of incarceration and arrest rates, or the wealth gap, or the education gap, that they don't just spring up, but in fact, the legacy of hundreds of years of systematic discrimination against African-Americans and people of color."

He continued, "The second thing is to make sure that all of us try to reach out. And Bruce and I talk about this a lot in the podcast, being able to reach out to people who aren't like us and doing so with an open mind and an open heart and knowing that you have to learn about folks who are not like you and that sometimes may make you uncomfortable. But if you're only with people who agree with you, laugh at the same things you do, listen to the same music, then we're not gonna learn from each other and things aren't gonna get better."

The former president highlighted one more crucial solution, "And the third thing is, and this may be the trickiest thing, you know, for White folks not to feel overly defensive or embattled when there's a discussion about our legacy of racism in this society, that it's not necessarily an indictment on them personally, but rather history describes that they can be a part of solving. And on the part of Visual Minority folks or people of color, understanding that just because somebody may not be as knowledgeable or appreciate everything that you're going through, or know the history of discrimination in this country, that doesn't make them a bad person and that you have to be willing to both correct folks when they're off, but not condemn them and suggest that just because they didn't get things exactly the way you think they should, that that makes them a bad person, right? That willingness to be open to others, and give people the benefit of the doubt, I think is also part of the healing process, and the reckoning process that we are gonna have to go through."

Believe The Problem Can Be Solved

You have to believe the problem can be fixed through finding commonality in humanity, whether you are a Visual Minority or White-presenting. If we don't believe that racism can be solved, then there is no point in trying to do anything at all. The task might be daunting, and it might feel like it will take a long time before we would ever make headway, but we have to keep believing. It would not be plausible to imagine that we would stumble on a formula or solution that will take away what was deliberately built into the system overnight.

Yet, we cannot stop trying. Our little drops of intelligence and progress can end up becoming an ocean someday. Tackling racism is just like cutting a huge tree with an ax. The first few chops will not bring the tree down. You will have to persevere and keep cutting until you get to that point when the tree can no longer withstand your persistence. Of course, just like in the case of a person that is cutting trees, there would be times that you might be tired and feel like quitting. In some cases, you might have to go home and come back the second day to continue where you left off.

You might also have to stop sometimes and go and sharpen the ax so that you will be more effective. In the same way, in this battle against racism, we would have to persevere to win the battle eventually. We would have to go back to the drawing board sometimes and seek better and more effective strategies that can help us to achieve monumental results. We would need more of the kind of energy that was seen during the Black Lives Matter protest, at different crucial points, to give us the platform for dialogue to land crucial blows.

The accumulation of several efforts over the years would eventually help us to get to that point when it is obvious that racism is a serious problem that has to be eradicated from our society. We need to get to that point when no racist would be able to hide anywhere because it is no longer acceptable, either explicitly or implicitly, to treat people wrongly based on their skin color. Until then, we need every White-presenting person that is not racist to make their voice heard. It is a collective effort from both sides of the divide that can get us to our promised land.

Appreciation Of Diversity

It's easier said than done, but you have to convert fear and rage from cultural differences, into curiosity and celebration of cultural differences. The fact that we have different races and cultures is not supposed to be a problem. It is supposed to be something beautiful every human should appreciate. I don't think anyone has issues with the fact that there are different fruits in the world. Diversity is beautiful if only we see the uniqueness in people. In a football team, the reason a team works well is when it has different players with different characteristics that can add value to it.

The defenders can tackle and recover the ball, while the attackers are adept at getting into goal-scoring positions and scoring goals. They are all important to the team. The team will crumble when the defenders want to act as attackers and when attackers try to do the jobs of defenders. My point is that diversity is a beautiful thing. There are various kinds of flowers in the world and they are all beautiful in their own way. There is nothing wrong with the fact that there are different people from different races that have different cultures in the world.

We should celebrate diversity because, at the end of the day, we all belong to the same human race. In *Black Lives*

Matter, Dax said, *"Change is what we really need. Cut me open, cut you open, red's the color, every human being bleeds. Let's come together, cops, citizens, and in between, and rally for the rights of everybody in humanity. Black, blue, white, green, playing for the same team."*

I know I have quoted this before, but the emphasis is different this time. This time, I am trying to point your attention to the part when he said, "Cut me open, cut you open, red's the color, every human being bleeds." This is the reality. It doesn't matter whether you are a Visual Minority or White-presenting. At the end of the day, we are all human beings who bleed. We need more White-presenting people that have a racial discrimination mindset to understand this. We all belong to the same human race, and the fact that we have strengths and weaknesses shouldn't be used against one another.

Genuine Friendship And Inclusion

White-presenting people need to make Visual Minority friends. I cannot say this enough. Of course, some White-presenting people try to do this but some of them go about it hypocritically. If you are a White-presenting person trying to make Visual Minority friends, you should want to get close to them in such a way that you can even confide in them. You should be able to have them over for dinner because you like them, and not because you're trying to prove you're not racist. This is where certain White-presenting people that try to get close to Visual Minority people get it wrong.

In some cases, the simulation of love is obvious. It sometimes feels as though a rich politician is relating to poor people on the street to earn points that will boost his political ambition. We all want to be accepted and not tolerated. When a Visual Minority notices that you are only trying to get close to him or her because you are trying to prove that you are not a racist, it is natural that he or she will want to withdraw from you. The truth is that you cannot pretend for long. If you don't judge a Visual Minority by pretending, what you think of them will soon be picked up.

If this applies to you, they will soon find out that your love and friendship are not genuine and that hurts. It is better not to try to get close to a person in the first place than to get close to them when you don't care about them. This pattern is relatively common, and it needs to stop. It is okay to take your time until you are sure that you are ready to express friendly gestures to more Visual Minority people. Until you are ready to do that, don't start a fake conversation. You will not be able to sustain it and it will be obvious in no time that you are pretending.

Once you are ready, start reaching out to one person at a time. Of course, you don't have to travel around looking for a Visual Minority that can be your friend.

More Open And Honest Conversations

Visual Minority people need to try to identify and trust the White-presenting people who reach out to them in genuine friendship (as rare as that is) and be patient with them and educate them about the receiving end of racism, without using understandable rage. Barack Obama pointed out this crucial point in his response to how racism can be solved in America. 'As a Visual Minority, I am always angry and disappointed whenever I read about all the wickedness that was perpetrated against Visual Minority slaves during the slave trade era. The dehumanization is often too overwhelming for me to handle, and this is how every Visual Minority feels when they are aware of the things that happened during that period.'

So, if this applies to you, our rage and annoyance are understandable and White-presenting people should also understand that. Yet, we must channel our energy in the right direction. It is the ancestral White-presenting people that enslaved our ancestors and the ones that are still racist today that should be our enemies. We shouldn't be unnecessarily aggressive towards the White-presenting people that are willing to reach out to us to have open and honest conversations. Some will indeed do it hypocritically just to score cheap points that they are not racists. Still, we should not assume that every White-presenting person that reaches out to us is like that.

We should be able to give people the benefit of the doubt. I have a culture of giving people the opportunity to prove themselves before I judge them. If we don't do this to the White-presenting people that try to know us and understand our pain, then we have become guilty of the same things we accuse White supremacists of doing. We should not categorize all White-presenting people as racists or hypocrites. I have had some really good White-presenting friends over the years. This could not have been possible if I was not willing to allow them to become a part of my life because they care about me.

Acceptance And Not Tolerance

More empathetic conversations between White-presenting people and Visual Minority people on an individual level, calm, and insightful story-telling level, must happen more often and permanently. This is vital because we all have to share this world and simply smiling at each other is not enough. More work needs to be done on the part of both sides to accept one another without any form of racial prejudice. Visual Minority people shouldn't assume anything about White-presenting people they meet until they have proven themselves genuine. Visual Minority people shouldn't see every White person as an individual that is trying to dismiss him or her to control the situation.

In the same way, White-presenting people should be willing to accept Visual Minority people on a basis other than their skin color, as their character. It would be hypocritical to expect a White-presenting person to be the friend of every Visual Minority he meets. I present as a Visual Minority, but every Visual Minority cannot be my friend. I have to observe the way a person behaves and their value system before they can be a part of my life and vice versa. However, what should never happen is when a person feels that another human being can never be his or her friend because of their race.

We need to start a new world where skin color or race is never the basis for judging people but only the qualities they possess are. This new beginning can only be achieved when we start looking beyond ethnicity and give people the benefit of the doubt. Tolerance is not enough. We should wholeheartedly accept that all races are equal. It should never be something that should be debatable on whatever basis. It is this agreement that will make us see ourselves as the same human race regardless of our ethnicity and skin color.

THANKS & CLOSING MESSAGE

What a journey we have had! I understand that it has been emotionally testing at times, but it was necessary to take that approach to wake us up and galvanize us towards taking necessary steps towards bringing an end to racism. To be honest, it hurts me whenever anyone, whether a Visual Minority or people who present as White, is not interested in contributing their fair share towards bringing an end to this problem. Visual Minority people are indeed the direct victims of racism, but you will also be affected at some point as a White-presenting person if we continue to have frustrated and angry Visual Minority people in our society. We cannot move forward if we avoid or dismiss each other's stories of inequity. We must have safer and more peaceful antiracist dialogues with others who do not look like us.

So, in my mind, what is best for us all is that we should come together under the same umbrella as the human race to overcome this common mission. I have attempted to do my small part by writing this book to inspire more people to be involved in ending racism.

Please, consider this book an invitation to be part of the movement to eliminate racism in your life. My hope while putting this material together is that it would inspire more people to see racism as a serious problem, one we need to tackle as soon as possible around the world.

If this book has inspired you to stop being racially ignorant, or racially neutral, and has put you on the path to becoming an antiracist, then my aim has been achieved. Beyond that conviction, I hope to see a better America, Canada, Britain, and other nations of the world where people are treated with equal dignity and respect, regardless of their skin color.

To me, racism is an invisible disease attacking the soul of humanity, and humanity's unrealized multicultural dialogue is the path to a cure. Remember, the words we use can either heal, or they can hurt, so we must use our words wisely. I feel privileged to have been a part of this journey with you.

Finally, to my intelligent and curious reader: Thank you for investing your time, energy, attention, and money into this project. But most of all, thank you for taking this sincere and imperfect journey with me – with this book, it has been my intention and my honor to explore the invisibility of racism to inspire more people around the world to simply get to know each other as humans.

- Long live the human race! - It's a great day to be alive!

Discovery Interviews From Visual Minority And Visual Majority People

Even though this sample of people is small, I spent hours with each person. I went deep into their stories and experiences. I asked them all the same questions but divided the group up into those who presented as White versus those who did not. It was my little experiment and I ensured that I had a control group to ensure that the participants don't give opinions based on what they felt they are expected to say but based on what they think.

BIPOC Interviews

S/S Interview

In this interview, I spoke with two people at once, their answers to the same questions are seen below:

Qs: Where were your parents born?

S/S: Guyana

Qs: Did you grow up with Visual Minority people in your neighborhood?

S/S: Yes/Not really.

Qs: If so, what did you learn about their culture from being around them?

S/S: Friends/Nobody talked about diversity; White-presenting people didn't show their diverse culture to us.

Qs: Have you ever had any Visual Minority friends or interracial relationships?

S/S: Yes/yes

Qs: Have you ever used the professional services of any Visual Minority people in your life (doctors, lawyers, etc.)?

S/S: Yes, but never thought about it/Yes

Qs: Have you ever thought about how you ethnically identify?

S/S: Yes/yes

Qs: How do you ethnically identify yourself?

S/S: Trinidadian, Jamaican / Guyanese, Indian but I identify originally as Indian.

Qs: How do you think society ethnically identifies you?

S/S: Indian / Indian

Qs: How would you define racism to someone who's never felt racist oppression before?

S/S: Feeling accepted in one part of the world only / Feeling accepted only among your race

Qs: What do you know about the 1700s history of racism?

S/S: In school, they never talked about it; there was no mention of minority racism or culture / Not much. Still don't know.

Qs: Have you heard of the wealth/education gap?

S/S: Not really / no.

Qs: Do you think white privilege and white entitlement exist?

S/S: Yes / Yes

Qs: Do you think BIPOC privilege & BIPOC entitlement exists?

S/S: No, but I think so / Yes for now. Even going too far.

Qs: Do you think you've socially benefited in any way from presenting as BIPOC?

S/S: No / Yes but only around diverse exotic circles.

Qs: How does racism affect you personally?

S/S: I don't like hearing about people being picked on / It makes me really sad. Struggling growing up with it felt unacceptable.

Qs: Are you more comfortable with BIPOC authority figures or white authority figures (police, doctors, lawyers, teachers, etc.) why?

S/S: Yes because Visual Minority people can get a sense of similar connection and sympathy / Yes because Visual Minority people have similar cultural values, relate, and understand me better.

Qs: Why do you think the topic of racism is unspoken and uncomfortable for some people?

S/S: Protection from pain to not be racist, irrelevant to their life, or maybe it brings a negative emotion out of them. / People don't realize racism is a personal experience - if it doesn't affect you, you don't talk about it.

Qs: What do you think perpetuates racism?

S/S: History, segregation, or people. / Wealth gap and people.

Qs: Do you think there could be a solution to racism?

S/S: Yes. It can't be gone but it would be a whole lot better through education because racism is made up of a lot of untrue facts. / It's possible but there's no single answer. I don't think it's likely based on the fact that it only takes one bad apple to spoil the bunch.

R Interview

Qs: Where were your parents born?

R: India

Qs: Did you grow up with Visual Minority people in your neighborhood? If so, what did you learn about their culture from being around them?

R: Yes. We don't have White-presenting people as such in India.

Qs: Have you ever had any Visual Minority friends or interracial relationships?

R: Yes.

Qs: Have you ever used the professional services of any Visual Minority people in your life (doctors, lawyers, etc.)?

R: Yes.

Qs: Have you ever thought about how you ethnically identify?

R: No.

Qs: How do you ethnically identify yourself?

R: I'm south Asian.

Qs: How do you think society ethnically identifies you?

R: Brown Indian Guy

Qs: How would you define racism to someone who's never felt racist oppression before?

R: Racism starts with your looks and your talk and lifestyle. It is more of society treating you unfairly because you are different.

Qs: What do you know about the 1700s history of racism?

R: Not much. I only know about British colonization and Black slavery to serve White-presenting people.

Qs: Have you heard of the wealth/education gap?

R: No.

Qs: What do you know of this?

R: Poorer get poorer and richer get richer In India, causing crime. In India, the British people took our gold and the Kohinoor diamond but they won't give it back. You can see it in their museums.

Qs: Do you think white privilege and white entitlement exist?

R: Of course I do.

Qs: Do you think BIPOC privilege & BIPOC entitlement exists?

R: No.

Qs: Do you think you've benefited in any way from presenting as BIPOC?

R: No. Not so far.

Qs: How does racism affect you personally?

R: It hasn't so far.

Qs: Are you more comfortable with BIPOC authority figures or white authority figures (police, doctors, lawyers, teachers, etc.) why?

R: More comfortable with VM. I don't know why the visual majority are overconfident compared to social norms in India.

Qs: Why do you think the topic of racism is unspoken and uncomfortable for people?

R: Because nobody accepts it. Racists never admit to racism.

Qs: What do you think perpetuates racism?

R: Hate.

Qs: Do you think there could be a solution to racism?

R: Yes but we have to look beyond skin color and geography.

H Interview

Qs: Where were your parents born?

H: Angola

Qs: Did you grow up with Visual Minority people in your neighborhood? If so, what did you learn about their culture from being around them?

H: Yes. Some of them see white folks as intelligent, protective of their culture, affluent, have easy access to better food, and are condescending.

Qs: Have you ever had any white friends or interracial relationships?

H: Yes.

Qs: Have you ever used the professional services of any Visual Minority people in your life (doctors, lawyers, etc.)?

H: Yes.

Qs: Have you ever thought about how you ethnically identify?

H: Yes.

Qs: How do you ethnically identify yourself?

H: Angolan.

Qs: How do you think society ethnically identifies you?

H: Black, funny guy. Not as intelligent.

Qs: How would you define racism to someone who's never felt racist oppression before?

H: When anybody looks at you and judges you negatively based on your skin color and denies you access to things.

Qs: What do you know about the history of racism?

H: Police brutality, slavery, back of the bus, and segregation.

Qs: Have you heard of the wealth/education gap?

H: Yes.

Qs: What do you know of this?

H: Some people took advantage of other people's resources and the wealth accumulated over time created distance between groups. Certain people have access to education unfairly.

Qs: Do you think white privilege and white entitlement exist?

H: Most definitely.

Qs: Do you think BIPOC privilege & BIPOC entitlement exists?

H: It may as a recent consequence of backlashes against modern-day racism and commitment to diversifying the workforce.

Qs: Do you think you've benefited in any way from presenting as BIPOC?

H: No. I don't have enough access to privileges.

Qs: How does racism affect you personally?

H: Many ways, especially emotionally.

Qs: Why?

H: When traveling to South Africa, treatment was different; you have to feel it. They act as though you are dirt.

Qs: Are you more comfortable with BIPOC authority figures or white authority figures (police, doctors, lawyers, teachers etc.) why?

H: It depends on how they portray themselves. I used to see White-presenting people as more intelligent. Now skin color doesn't matter.

Qs: Why do you think the topic of racism is unspoken and uncomfortable for people?

H: It's emotional. It's defensive, triggering discomfort.

Qs: What do you think perpetuates racism?

H: Financial gain and differential advantage.

Qs: Do you think there could be a solution to racism?

H: Yes. Equality. Equal access to resources. You have to provide equality.

N Interview

Qs: Where were your parents born?

N: Pakistan

Qs: Did you grow up with Visual Minority people in your neighborhood? If so, what did you learn about their culture from being around them?

N: Yes. Everyone's different and that was normal. Everyone was represented in my neighborhood. Kids playing together were from all ethnicities.

Qs: Have you ever had any Visual Minority friends or interracial relationships?

N: Yes

Qs: Have you ever used the professional services of any Visual Minority people in your life (doctors, lawyers, etc.)?

N: Yes

Qs: Have you ever thought about how you ethnically identify?

N: Somewhat.

Qs: How do you ethnically identify yourself?

N: As a Canadian with East Indian heritage.

Qs: How do you think society ethnically identifies you?

N: I don't know racially; people see me as gritty and scrappy (from a lower class).

Qs: How would you define racism to someone who's never felt racist oppression before?

N: Racism is the negative result of incorrect assumptions based on visible body features.

Qs: What do you know about the history of racism?

N: Stems back to tribalism. The origin of all the wars comes from defending their people and class, needing more resources.

Qs: Have you heard of the wealth/education gap?

N: Not really and yes.

Qs: What do you know of this?

N: Generational wealth creates a systemic advantage. Those without advantage are on the other end of the spectrum.

Qs: Do you think white privilege and white entitlement exist?

N: Yes.

Qs: Do you think BIPOC privilege & BIPOC entitlement exists?

N: Yes.

Qs: Do you think you've benefited in any way from presenting as BIPOC?

N: Locally, no. Globally, yes.

Qs: Expand.

N: Globally, I've traveled to 40 countries. I blend into other Visual Minority people in other countries. Locally, no. Many people around me are racially ignorant. When I'm working in my yard, people think I'm the laborer, not the owner. Not taken seriously. I am also disadvantaged in the business world because I'm visually different.

Qs: How does racism affect you personally?

N: It's an everyday aspect of my life. It isn't visible. I don't think people appreciate how real it is. I play online video games, and I can't believe how many people drop the N-word. Racism is just under the surface. How do you ignore the fact that Visual Minority people are being killed by cops every day?

Qs: Are you more comfortable with BIPOC authority figures or white authority figures (police, doctors, lawyers, teachers, etc.) why?

N: I don't know.

Qs: Expand.

N: A lot of minorities carry with them racist baggage. In India, lighter skin became part of the definition of beauty based on colonial-controlled countries. So, this interferes with how we see experts.

Qs: Why do you think the topic of racism is unspoken and uncomfortable for many people?

N: Because there's not an awareness of their views. It's so ingrained and subconscious. They have been programmed to see people a certain way.

Qs: What do you think perpetuates racism?

N: Doubling down on tribalism.

Qs: Do you think there could be a solution to racism?

N: Yes, several solutions. Time. Don't be passive; correct the racism you see to help deprogram racism. As the population increases and mixes and waters down tribalism, global disasters bring people together, having a single global mindset for growing populations, and something that forces us to come together. It won't happen naturally.

F Interview

Qs: Where were your parents born?

F: China. They grew up in Taiwan.

Qs: Did you grow up with Visual Minority people in your neighborhood? If so, what did you learn about their culture from being around them?

F: Yeah! The difference with food.

Qs: Have you ever had any Visual Minority friends?

F: No. interracial relationships? Yes.

Qs: Have you ever used the professional services of any Visual Minority people in your life (doctors, lawyers, etc.)?

F: Yes.

Qs: Have you ever thought about how you ethnically identify?

F: No

Qs: How do you ethnically identify yourself?

F: Chinese but the values are Canadian.

Qs: How do you think society ethnically identifies you?

F: Chinese.

Qs: How would you define racism to someone who's never felt racist oppression before?

F: Challenging to do. Something you experience that has nothing to do with anything except your visual identity.

Qs: What do you know about the history of racism?

F: Slavery, railroads, and internment camps.

Qs: Have you heard of the wealth/education gap?

F: Yes.

Qs: What do you know of this?

F: As a Chinese person, the stereotype works to my advantage. Being educated opens doors for me.

Qs: Do you think white privilege and white entitlement exist?

F: Yes.

Qs: Do you think BIPOC privilege & BIPOC entitlement exists?

F: No. But there is a stack rank due to skin color. The Asian community is embarrassingly racist to Visual Minority people.

Qs: Do you think you've benefited in any way from presenting as BIPOC?

F: I don't know

Qs: Expand.

F: I was not penalized for presenting as a BIPOC.

Qs: How does racism affect you personally?

F: It comes out of nowhere.

Qs: Are you more comfortable with BIPOC authority figures or white authority figures (police, doctors, lawyers, teachers, etc.)? Why?

F: Can't give a straight answer. I am careful. I never had a problem.

Qs: Why do you think the topic of racism is unspoken and uncomfortable for people?

F: You have to account for your racial ignorance. Uncomfortable, especially if you have experienced it. You need safety to talk about it because it's very personal.

Qs: What do you think perpetuates racism?

F: Probably not talking about it and avoiding those conversations. Society is slow to change.

Qs: Do you think there could be a solution to racism?

F: Yes.

Qs: Expand.

F: Education, exposure, tolerance, and integration.

H Interview

Qs: Where were your parents born?

H: Syria.

Qs: Did you grow up with Visual Minority people in your neighborhood?

H: No.

Qs: What did you learn about their white culture from being around them in Canada?

H: I perceived white families as having clear physical and emotional boundaries - they valued education - everyone was reading.

Qs: Have you ever had any Visual Minority friends?

H: Yes, it took a while for that to happen until I moved to Toronto.

Qs: Have you ever used the professional services of any Visual Minority people in your life (doctors, lawyers, etc.)?

H: Yes.

Qs: Have you ever thought about how you ethnically identify?

H: Yes, it has crossed my mind.

Qs: How do you ethnically identify yourself?

H: Levantine Arab. Syrian and Canadian sometimes. I didn't want to talk about my Syrian identity, but now I do.

Qs: How do you think society ethnically identifies you?

H: Generally, people perceive me as white. Some say I'm Jewish. When they hear my name, they know I'm Middle Eastern.

Qs: How would you define racism to someone who's never felt racist oppression before?

H: Racist people consider themselves as better and smarter than others based on the color of their skin, where they grew up, and the origins of their name. It is a behavior that is immoral that I don't identify with and should not exist.

Qs: What do you know about the North American history of racism from the 1700s to the modern-day?

H: Slavery, normalizing murder, rape, and stealing land. Visual Minority experience is the prominent one. I have less exposure to other forms of racism like Aboriginal racism. I don't have a robust knowledge of racist history.

Qs: Have you heard of the wealth/education gap?

H: Yes.

Qs: What do you know of this?

H: In the US, there was a movement to create equality. Logically, there are people at a disadvantage in education from being from poor generations.

Qs: Do you think white privilege and white entitlement exist?

H: Yes, I didn't think about it as much. I'm becoming more aware of it.

Qs: Do you think BIPOC privilege & BIPOC entitlement exists?

H: It should exist.

Qs: Do you think you've benefited in any way from presenting as light-skinned BIPOC

H: If I did, I wasn't aware of it.

Qs: Expand.

H: In Syria, skin shade is a factor. Lighter skin is more valuable.

Qs: How does racism affect you personally?

H: When I was a new immigrant, people made fun of me. I refused to admit racism exists in Canada but I know it does. Maybe I could have moved up in my career faster if I had a white-sounding name. It's annoying to simplify my name so that visual majorities can pronounce and remember my name.

Qs: Are you more comfortable with BIPOC authority figures or white authority figures (police, doctors, lawyers, teachers etc.)?

H: I haven't thought about this. I would feel more comfortable around more BIPOC figures.

Qs: Why? Expand.

H: I have a feeling a Visual Minority cop would treat me better than a white cop by instinct alone based on a Visual Minority cop having to overcome racist issues on their own, which would make a Visual Minority cop behave a certain way. But I haven't had enough interaction to know for sure.

Qs: Why do you think the topic of racism is unspoken and uncomfortable for people?

H: People are worried about triggering people. Maybe people are waiting for permission from others to discuss it with others. Lack of familiarity is also a factor.

Qs: What do you think perpetuates racism?

H: False assumptions without validation.

Qs: Do you think there could be a solution to racism?

H: There could be, but there is an inherent propensity for people to be unfair to others.

Qs: Expand.

H: I think it will always be there. There will always be people who think they are better. Maybe it's like natural selection, where racist people will be outnumbered and out-evolved by anti-racist people, but I'm a utopian optimist.

White-Presenting Interviews

Z Interview. (Public - not anonymous)

Qs: Where was your mother/father born?

Z: Ontario.

Qs: Did you grow up with Visual Minority people in your neighborhood? If so, what did you learn about their culture from being around them?

Z: Yes. I don't know. It was a predominantly white community. Each street had its hockey team in a school of 1500. Maybe 40 identified as Visual Minority. At 18

279

years old, I was exposed to different cultures. We never thought about it that much. I would like to go back and talk to minorities about their experience living with visual majorities. I was oblivious to race and racial challenges.

Qs: Have you ever had any Visual Minority friends or interracial relationships?

Z: Many

Qs: Have you ever used the services of any Visual Minority people in your life (doctors, lawyers, etc.).

Z: Yes.

Qs: Have you ever thought about how you ethnically identify?

Z: Yes

Qs: How do you ethnically identify yourself?

Z: Canadian 1st with British roots

Qs: How do you think society ethnically identifies you?

Z: They know I'm from Canada when they hear me speak.

Qs: How would you define racism to someone who's never felt racist oppression before?

Z: It's a negative judgment on an individual based on appearance.

Qs: What do you know about the history of racism?

Z: In 1792, people couldn't bring slaves to Canada. Jim Crow laws, Underground Railroad, Visual Minority community in Nova Scotia, racist laws in Canada indigenous, Japanese internment, etc.

Qs: Have you heard of the wealth/education gap?

Z: Yes.

Qs: What do you know of this?

Z: Disproportionate social capital for Visual Minority people.

Qs: Do you think white privilege and white entitlement exist?

Z: Oh god yeah.

Qs: Do you think you've benefited in any way from presenting as white?

Yes.

Qs: Expand.

Z: So many ways. Due to my white hair, people call me sir. I didn't understand white privilege but now I understand. People help me a lot more (noticed this in India) because I'm white.

Qs: Have you ever spoken to, or listened to a Visual Minority before about their thoughts and feelings of racism affecting them?

Z: Yes.

Qs: How does racism affect you personally?

Z: I assumed society would increase its social mobility since I went to school. Over the last 30 years, the Visual

Minority people never got the opportunities the middle class has by dividing and conquering via racism. Why?

Qs: Why do you think the topic of racism is unspoken and uncomfortable for many people?

Z: I think we are all afraid of making a mistake and offending someone.

Qs: What do you think perpetuates racism?

Z: I think it's a sense of protective mechanism when people feel they are under threat. People are looking for someone else to identify with. Politicians feed off that.

Qs: Do you think there could be a solution to racism?

Z: I think you can certainly reduce racism. We have come a long way in Canada; I don't think you can stamp it out. But it takes conscious effort.

T Interview

Qs: Where was your mother/father born?

T: Mom Italy, dad Toronto

Qs: Did you grow up with Visual Minority people in your neighborhood? If so, what did you learn about their culture from being around them?

T: Yes. A lot of Italians and Visual Minority people. Not sure.

Qs: Have you ever had any Visual Minority friends or interracial relationships?

T: No.

Qs: Have you ever used the professional services of any Visual Minority people in your life (doctors, lawyers, etc.)?

T: No.

Qs: Have you ever thought about how you ethnically identify?

T: Yes.

Q: How do you ethnically identify yourself?

T: I'm supposed to identify as White. I always thought white meant WASP (White Anglo-Saxon Protestants) (that's not me).

Qs: How do you think society ethnically identifies you?

T: White, but WASP thinks 'other.'

Qs: How would you define racism to someone who's never felt racist oppression before?

T: It's not about who you are; it's about the way you look - some people aren't going to think you matter, or won't give you a job, and they won't get to know you because of your skin color.

Qs: What do you know about the history of racism from the 1700s to now?

T: Slavery. Christopher Columbus was more a soldier than an explorer. Kinky hair meant you were black. Underground Railroad from the US to Canada.

Qs: Have you heard of the wealth/education gap?

T: Rings a bell.

Qs: What do you know of this?

T: Something to do with Visual Minority people's lower education or higher dropout rates, being paid less, etc.

Qs: Do you think White privilege and White entitlement exist?

T: I'm sure they do. Privilege means people don't discriminate against you because you're white.

Qs: Do you think you've benefited in any way from presenting as white?

T: Yes. My name makes me sound non-threatening.

Qs: Have you ever spoken to, or listened to a Visual Minority before about their thoughts and feelings of racism affecting them?

T: I don't think so. Read some articles.

Qs: How does racism affect you personally?

T: Maybe I'm mostly ignorant. I don't know.

Qs: Why do you think the topic of racism is unspoken and uncomfortable for some White-presenting people?

T: Nobody wants to think they are racist. I wonder if it's because it opens up a can of worms that forces all these feelings and assumptions and work, and most people don't want to do that work. They don't do that kind of reflection work in their own lives. Most people don't have good emotional health and language.

Qs: What do you think perpetuates racism?

T: Handed-down beliefs. Racism is still unexamined. Visual Minority people are bearing the brunt of people then get written off and dismissed before they are heard. The divide just grows without dialogue.

Qs: Do you think there could be a solution to racism?

T: There is a solution to everything. So, there has to be a solution to move forward.

Qs: Expand.

T: It's everybody's problem. I feel the popular topic today is that all the power to change racism is 100% in the hands of White-presenting people only. Racism solutions need to be more evenly spread. If you have white privilege, you can use it to help others. Connect with someone, start by just saying hello to someone outside of your ethnicity.   Categories of people that are being painted with these broad brushes don't make sense to me.

L Interview

Qs: Where was your mother/father born?

L: Poland father. Toronto mother.

Qs: Did you grow up with Visual Minority people in your neighborhood? If so, what did you learn about their culture from being around them?

L: Yes. Lots of racial diversity on my street. Racial diversity didn't register as an issue. Learned a bit about the Muslim religion. I observed Kids' interaction with their strict Chinese parents. The parents were friendly. No racist issues.

Qs: Have you ever had any Visual Minority friends?

L: Yes.

Qs: Have you ever used the professional services of any Visual Minority people in your life (doctors, lawyers, etc.)?.

L: Yes, doctors.

Qs: Have you ever thought about how you ethnically identify?

L: I don't know. No.

Qs: How do you ethnically identify yourself?

L: Eastern European Jewish.

Qs: How do you think society ethnically identifies you?

L: White. I don't have a stereotypical look.

Qs: How would you define racism to someone who's never felt racist oppression before?

L: Imagine somebody didn't like you because of how you looked.

Qs: What do you know about the 1700s history of racism?

L: Black slavery, Jewish persecution, and East Indian caste system. I understand where it comes from. Maybe fear. People being tribal who were territorial - stems from primitive instincts.

Qs: Have you heard of the wealth/education gap?

L: Yes.

Qs: What do you know of this?

L: The distributions of wealth among White-presenting people and Visual Minority people are not equal due to slavery. However, the great majority is that people have to take responsibility for themselves.

Qs: Do you think white privilege and white entitlement exist?

L: Yes, but it's a bit complicated. I don't think it applies as a blanket statement. I suppose a minority will have a disadvantage. There must be an advantage to being white. Is it quantifiable?

Qs: Do you think you've benefited in any way from presenting as white?

L: I don't know. It's hard for me to say. It's possible.

Qs: Have you ever spoken to, or listened to a Visual Minority before about their thoughts and feelings of racism affecting them?

L: Yes but it hasn't been super deep.

Qs: How does racism affect you personally?

L: I don't know. I'm emotionally conflicted because people don't walk around thinking about it. It's a matter of personal experience. I haven't had to deal with that day-to-day.

Qs: Why do you think the topic of racism is unspoken and uncomfortable for some White-presenting people?

L: Conversation isn't allowed about anything these days, it seems. We are all living in fear about what to say because of judgment.

Qs: What do you think perpetuates racism?

L: The fact that we feel we can't talk about it openly. Media expressing the worst parts of any culture is also a factor.

Qs: Do you think there could be a solution to racism?

Yes. Not overnight.

Qs: Expand.

L: Education and exposure from a young age to different cultures and ideas and acceptance. People have generational rage. We all have to let go of the anger with open conversation, coming to mutual understanding.

B Interview

Qs: Where was your mother/father born?

B: Dad, America, mom, Canada

Qs: Did you grow up with Visual Minority People in your neighborhood? If so, what did you learn about their culture from being around them?

B: Yes. Lived in Africa for 6-7 years. It gave me a broad perspective of global culture. Learned about culture living in Africa for six years but still felt like a spectator going to the food markets, safari, rural grass huts, watching kids playing with a tire rim and coat hangers, then moving to northern Canada with only one Visual Minority kid. Hard to experience culture unless you live in it. In Africa, the community raises the child; in NA, it's the family who raises the child.

Qs: Have you ever had any Visual Minority friends or interracial relationships?

B: Yes.

Qs: Have you ever used the services of any BIPOC professional people in your life (doctors, lawyers etc.).

B: Yes. Raised by a Visual Minority nanny and her kids.

Qs: Have you ever thought about how you ethnically identify?

B: Yes, I suppose.

Qs: How do you ethnically identify yourself?

B: Definitely white, but I worry about how it makes Visual Minority people feel. Sometimes I see the apprehension in Visual Minority people when they see me. I worry people are threatened by me because I'm white.

Qs: How do you think society ethnically identifies you?

B: White, privileged, a bit entitled.

Qs: How would you define racism to someone who's never felt racist oppression before?

B: Hating someone for their skin color and not for who they are.

Qs: What do you know about the 1700s history of racism?

B: Colonial Spain/England taking people forcibly from their homes to work for them. Locally, they took native Indians from their homes and tried to break them of their cultural heritage.

Qs: Have you heard of the wealth/education gap?

B: Yes.

Qs: What do you know of this?

B: A form of suppression, ensuring people don't rise above a certain level of status. Originally done through controlling wealth and now education and politics. For example, suppressing the vote and the ability to change the laws so you can't qualify for jobs and get an education. Some people just give up and turn to drugs and break the law to survive. That system hasn't changed since European castes' days.

Qs: Do you think white privilege and white entitlement exist?

B: Yes. I don't think anybody asks for it or expects it consciously. If you were born into wealth, you were entitled. The caste system is still there and most people don't recognize it. It's generational; the expectations are passed through the generation.

Qs: Do you think you've benefited in any way from presenting as white?

B: Yes.

Qs: Expand.

B: On a daily basis, I get pulled over - I get off while Visual Minority people can get their vehicle searched. There is a difference in the way people are treated.

Qs: Have you ever spoken to, or listened to Visual Minority people before about their thoughts and feelings of racism affecting them?

B: Yes. Learned their perspective on fear (how afraid they are on a regular basis) and apprehension about how they will be treated. I don't expect a cop to pull me out of my car when I get pulled over; I expect a warning, realizing the system is unfair.

Qs: How does racism affect you personally?

B: It has affected me; some people assume I'm the norm. I tried to become a cop, and they said white males need not apply. But I've never been threatened.

Qs: Why do you think the topic of racism is unspoken and uncomfortable for some White-presenting people?

B: People don't want to feel stupid, it's their fault, and people don't want to admit their limitations, embarrassment, not wanting to admit your weaknesses.

Qs: What do you think perpetuates racism?

B: Fear and lack of experience in other cultures face to face with people.

Qs: Do you think there could be a solution to racism?

B: Yes.

Qs: Expand.

B: Sharing cultural experiences face to face helps you become more culturally aware. You have to be willing to step outside your comfort level and share your life with Visual Minority people. Go for coffee with someone, spend time with them, and talk to them. Life is busy but it's not complicated. You must slow down and take the time to talk to people.

Qs: Cause of racism

B: Hate or ignorance (maybe fear of supremacy)

Qs: Other

B: Hate rooted in fear. The system in North America is created more for White-presenting people than Visual Minority people. Systemic racism is about people's obliviousness to racism, meaning awareness can evolve it. People need to be welcomed into other cultures. To those who are new to the invisibility of inequality, open yourself up to get to know other people.

An Interview

Qs: Where was your mother/father born?

A: Israel

Qs: Did you grow up with Visual Minority people in your neighborhood? If so, what did you learn about their culture from being around them?

A: One kid on my street from India. (Have to think hard). No - backyard play.

Qs: Have you ever had any Visual Minority friends or interracial relationships?

A: No. Knew a housekeeper we lived with.

Qs: Have you ever used the services of any Visual Minority people in your life (doctors, lawyers etc.).

A: Yes.

Qs: Have you ever thought about how you ethnically identify?

A: Canadian Jew - never felt a need to define it. As a business owner, I never felt the need to.

Qs: How do you think society ethnically identifies you?

A: Never thought of it - no reason to think of it. As a Jew, not as a white person - never encountered racism.

Qs: How would you define racism to someone who's never felt racist oppression before?

A: When people intentionally or unconsciously cause harm to others who are not like them because that's what they learned.

Qs: What do you know about the history of racism?

A: Know from experience from friends, employees, podcasts, and strife in Africa with Ethiopian Jews. I am aware of oriental Asians in Canada charged with building railroads, Japanese internment camps, WW2, slavery from Europe, and Africa, civil rights movement, rioting,

BLM, and destruction of property. Racism is not white vs. black.

Qs: Have you heard of the wealth/education gap?

A: Yes

Qs: What do you know of this?

A: If there is a low opportunity from birth, which has a greater likelihood to repeat itself. Families of poor backgrounds seem to have historically fewer opportunities.

Qs: Do you think white privilege and white entitlement exist?

A: It exists in the mind of the person who is not white. I am privileged but I don't think it's because I'm white. Not for me. Not for anyone else I know very well because of choices and merit.

Qs: Do you think you've benefited in any way from presenting as white?

A: No

Qs: Have you ever spoken to, or listened to a Visual Minority before about their thoughts and feelings of racism affecting them?

A: Yes.

Qs: How does racism affect you personally?

A: No way

Qs: Why?

A: I know I don't know everything. Interested in hearing other people's experiences.

Qs: Why do you think the topic of racism is unspoken and uncomfortable?

A: I don't think it is uncomfortable for me.

Qs: What do you think perpetuates racism?

A: Today - difference from a lot of other people can create anxiety. Single-parent families add pressure to the perpetuation of racism. A lot to do with how you are raised by family. In 1965/70, it was more us vs. them mentality. Lots of racist snobby people might make inappropriate comments in private.

Qs: Do you think there could be a solution to racism?

A: No.

Qs: Expand

A: Genetically, we are taught what is familiar. We are tribal, and we want to be with people who are like us and familiar. But it could become less acute over time.

L Interview

Qs: Where was your mother/father born?

L: Israel.

Qs: Did you grow up with Visual Minority people in your neighborhood? If so, what did you learn about their culture from being around them?

L: Initially, not many. Yes, not that many. Very little.

Qs: Have you ever had any Visual Minority friends or interracial relationships?

L: Yes. Relationship while traveling.

Qs: Have you ever used the services of any Visual Minority people in your life (doctors, lawyers etc.)?

L: Yes.

Qs: Have you ever thought about how you ethnically identify?

L: Yes

Qs: How do you ethnically identify yourself?

L: I know I look white, but more BIPOC.

Qs: How do you think society ethnically identifies you?

L: White

Qs: How would you define racism to someone who's never felt racist oppression before?

L: Difficult. I've had few racist experiences.

Qs: What do you know about the history of racism?

L: North America was a slave continent. 4 of 10 of it.

Qs: Have you heard of the wealth/education gap?

L: Yes.

Qs: What do you know of this?

L: There's a momentum for and against people. People who have wealth can have education and vice versa. You need money to make money but struggle because of invisible shackles.

Qs: Do you think white privilege and white entitlement exist?

L: Yes.

Qs: Do you think you've benefited in any way from presenting as white?

L: I don't really know the pain from racism.

Qs: Have you ever spoken to, or listened to a Visual Minority before about their thoughts and feelings of racism affecting them?

L: Yes.

Qs: How does racism affect you personally?

L: Very little. I'm awakening to something underneath my nose. I want to get it right.

Qs: Why do you think the topic of racism is unspoken and uncomfortable for White-presenting people?

L: Unearned power. They don't know they have the privilege.

Qs: What do you think perpetuates racism?

L: Denial, self-protection, fear, lack of understanding/experience, and compassion.

Qs: Do you think there could be a solution to racism?

L: Absolutely. Honest sharing and asking each other questions.

As a result of these interviews, in my mind, I confirmed this subject makes most people feel uncomfortable and some have difficulty articulating their experience, while others are sensitive in coming face to face with their lack of awareness and ignorance of the plight of others who have to calculate how to adapt to social norms originally designed by colonial influence. Others were shocked to learn how brutal being on the wrong side of racism can be and has been. On the other hand, some didn't know they were socially battle-fatigued. I became quickly aware that these people wanted to have these conversations but either needed the facilitation or the emotional space to be allowed to organize their raw thoughts and experiences.

From this small sample, I learned that inequity is barely understood ubiquitously because it cannot be felt equally. However, having a peaceful dialogue (based on genuine curiosity and respect) helps. I learned that some people who present as White (whose origins lay outside of Britain) feel mildly discriminated against (by those whose origins lay closer to Britain), which suggests to me that inequity runs deeper than I thought. I also learned that some Visual Minority people might not be aware that the subtleties of inequity tend to be aimed at them. And finally, I learned that some — no matter their cultural backgrounds -- are keenly aware that racism is all around us -- only that it has taken on a more clandestine form in the last 25 years in North America but is so easily noticeable in Asia today - you don't have to look for it.

References

Warren, C. (2017). *The gun-slave hypothesis and the 18th-century British slave trade -Munich Personal RePEc Archive.* Https://Mpra.Ub.Uni-Muenchen.de/80050/.
https://mpra.ub.uni-muenchen.de/80050/

Tim, E. (1970, August 22). *Emerging findings on the impact of COVID-19 on black and minority ethnic people.* The Health Foundation.
https://www.health.org.uk/news-and-comment/charts-and-infographics/emerging-findings-on-the-impact-of-covid-19-on-black-and-min

Siddique, H. (2020, August 25). *Key findings from Public Health England's report on Covid-19 deaths.* The Guardian.
https://www.theguardian.com/world/2020/jun/02/key-findings-from-public-health-englands-report-on-covid-19-deaths

Garcia, R., Ali, N., Papadopoulos, C. *et al.* Specific antenatal interventions for Black, Asian and Minority Ethnic (BAME) pregnant women at high risk of poor birth outcomes in the United Kingdom: a scoping review. *BMC Pregnancy Childbirth* **15,** 226 (2015). https://doi.org/10.1186/s12884-015-06 57-2

299

CPAG (2021) *Who is at risk of poverty?* CPAG.
https://cpag.org.uk/child-poverty/who-risk-poverty

Dunham, Y., Baron, A. S., & Carey, S. (2011).
Consequences of "minimal" group affiliations in
children. *Child Development, 82*(3), 793–811.
https://doi.org/10.1111/j.1467-8624.2011.01577.x

Sander F. (2020) *Seven factors contributing to American
racism*. Stanford News.
https://news.stanford.edu/2020/06/09/seven-factors-
contributing-american-racism/
Lynne, P. (2019). *What the data say about police
shootings*. Nature.
https://www.nature.com/articles/d41586-019-02601-
9

Harvard (2020) *Black people more than three times as
likely as White-presenting people to be killed during a
police encounter* News.
https://www.hsph.harvard.edu/news/hsph-in-the-
news/blacks-White-presenting people-police-deaths-
disparity/

Woodson, Carter G. (1918) *"The Beginnings of the
Miscegenation of the White-presenting people and
Blacks", The Journal of Negro History, 3 (4): 335–353,
doi:10.2307/2713814, JSTOR 2713814*

Fredrickson, George M. *(1987)*, *The Black Image in the White Mind*, Wesleyan University Press, p. *172*, ISBN *0-8195-6188-6*

Livingston, G., & Brown, A. (2020, May 30). *Intermarriage in the U.S. 50 Years After Loving v. Virginia*. Pew Research Center's Social & Demographic Trends Project. https://www.pewresearch.org/social-trends/2017/05/18/intermarriage-in-the-u-s-50-years-after-loving-v-virginia/

Mitchell, T. (2020, May 30). *1. Trends and patterns in intermarriage*. Pew Research Center's Social & Demographic Trends Project. https://www.pewresearch.org/social-trends/2017/05/18/1-trends-and-patterns-in-intermarriage/

Statistic Canada (2011). *Fifty years of families in Canada: 1961 to 2011*. https://www12.statcan.gc.ca/census-recensement/2011/as-sa/98-312-x/98-312-x2011003_1-eng.cfm

Partel, A. (2021, January 29). *15% of Canadians would never marry outside their race: Ipsos poll*. Global News. https://globalnews.ca/news/5297312/interracial-marriage-canada/

IPSOS. (2020). *Majority (60%) See Racism as a Serious Problem in Canada Today, Up 13 points Since Last Year*. IPSOS. https://www.ipsos.com/en-ca/majority-60-see-racism-serious-problem-canada-today-13-points-last-year

Pew Research. (2020, May 30). *Chapter 1: Overview*. Pew Research Center's Social & Demographic Trends Project. https://www.pewresearch.org/social-trends/2012/02/16/chapter-1-overview/

Fadulu, L. (2020, June 11). *Study Shows Income Gap Between Rich and Poor Keeps Growing, With Deadly Effects*. The New York Times. https://www.nytimes.com/2019/09/10/us/politics/gao-income-gap-rich-poor.html

Statista. (2021, August 9). *Breakdown of U.S. millionaires by race/ethnicity 2013*. https://www.statista.com/statistics/300528/us-millionaires-race-ethnicity/

Bursell, Moa. (2007). What's in a Name? A Field Experiment Test for the Existence of Ethnic Discrimination in the Hiring Process.

Jalen, R. (2015). *PolitiFact - Do job-seekers with "white" names get more callbacks than "black" names?* @politifact. https://www.politifact.com/factchecks/2015/mar/15/jalen-ross/black-name-resume-50-percent-less-likely-get-respo/

Smith, W., Hung, M., & Franklin, J. (2011). Racial Battle Fatigue and the MisEducation of Black Men: Racial Microaggressions, Societal Problems, and Environmental Stress. *The Journal of Negro Education, 80*(1), 63-82. Retrieved September 3, 2021, from http://www.jstor.org/stable/41341106

Russell M. Lawson; Benjamin A. Lawson *(11 October 2019). Race and Ethnicity in America: From Pre-contact to the Present [4 volumes].* ABC-CLIO. pp. 16–. *ISBN 978-1-4408-5097-4.*

Mary Ann Shadd (2016). *A Plea for Emigration; or Notes of Canada West: A Broadview Anthology of British Literature Edition.* Broadview Press. p. 11. *ISBN 978-1-55481-321-6.*

Howard-Hassmann, R. E. (2020, June 14). *Why reparations and apologies to African Canadians are necessary.* The Conversation. https://theconversation.com/why-reparations-and-apologies-to-african-canadians-are-necessary-140527

Anthony M. (2019) *What's wrong with a cheque? A call for slavery reparations in Canada.* Ricochet. https://ricochet.media/en/2554/whats-wrong-with-a-cheque-a-call-for-slavery-reparations-in-canada

The Canadian Encyclopedia. (2018). *Black History | The Canadian Encyclopedia.* Retrieved September 3, 2021, from https://www.thecanadianencyclopedia.ca/en/timeline/black-history

Ministry of International Trade. (2020, September 1). *History of wrongs towards B.C.'s Chinese Canadians - Province of British Columbia*. British Columbia. https://www2.gov.bc.ca/gov/content/governments/multiculturalism-anti-racism/chinese-legacy-bc/history

National Post Staff. (2020, June 11). *Who was Henry Dundas and why do two cities no longer want to honour his memory?* National post. https://nationalpost.com/news/world/who-was-henry-dundas-and-why-do-two-cities-no-longer-want-to-honour-his-memory

Luxen, Micah (June 24, 2016). *"Survivors of Canada's 'cultural genocide' still healing"*. BBC. *Archived* from the original on July 25, 2016. Retrieved June 28, 2016.

Milloy, John S. (1999). *A National Crime: The Canadian Government and the Residential School System, 1879 to 1986*. Critical Studies in Native History. **11**. *University of Manitoba Press*. *ISBN* *0-88755-646-9*.

Shapiro, Thomas M. (2004). *The Hidden Cost of Being African American*. New York: Oxford UP. pp. *33*. *ISBN* *978-0-19-518138-8*. The hidden cost of being African American.

Van Loo, Rory (1 January 2009). *"A Tale of Two Debtors: Bankruptcy Disparities by Race"*. Albany Law Review. ***72***: *231*.

Ewen, Lara (January–February 2021). *"Tarnished legacies: Presidential libraries grapple with the histories of their subjects"*. American Libraries. *Chicago:* American Library Association.

Hunter, T. W. (2019, April 16). *Opinion | When Slave Owners Got Reparations*. The New York Times. https://www.nytimes.com/2019/04/16/opinion/when-slaveowners-got-reparations.html

Fede, A. (1985). Legitimized Violent Slave Abuse in the American South, 1619-1865: A Case Study of Law and Social Change in Six Southern States. *The American Journal of Legal History, 29*(2), 93-150. doi:10.2307/844931

Library of Congress. (n.d.). *The Murder of Emmett Till | Articles and Essays | Civil Rights History Project | Digital Collections | Library of Congress*. The Library of Congress. Retrieved September 3, 2021, from https://www.loc.gov/collections/civil-rights-history-project/articles-and-essays/murder-of-emmett-till/

SocialWorker.com. (2015, September 28). *The Tuskegee Syphilis Study and Its Implications for the 21st Century*. https://www.socialworker.com/feature-

articles/ethicsarticles/The_Tuskegee_Syphilis_Study_an
d_Its_Implications_for_the_21st_Century/

Perdue, T. (1997). Columbus Meets Pocahontas in the
American South. *Southern Cultures, 3*(1), 4-21.
Retrieved September 3, 2021, from
http://www.jstor.org/stable/26235428

Ross, A. (2018, April 23). *How American Racism
Influenced Hitler*. The New Yorker.
https://www.newyorker.com/magazine/2018/04/30/
how-american-racism-influenced-hitler

National Archives. (2017, September 1). *Black Soldiers
in the U.S. Military During the Civil War*.
https://www.archives.gov/education/lessons/blacks-
civil-war

*DeNeed L. Brown (October 19, 2020). "Tulsa begins
search for 'Original 18' black people killed in 1921 race
massacre". The Washington Post.*

Horton, B. J. (2020, September 25). *George Floyd: What
has Trump done for black jobs, poverty and crime?* BBC
News. https://www.bbc.com/news/world-us-canada-
52907646

Thank you for reading this book!

If you found this book helpful, I would be grateful if you would **post an honest review on Amazon** so this book can reach other supportive readers like you!

All you need to do is digitally flip to the back and leave your review. Or visit amazon.com/author/senseipauldavid click the correct book cover and click on the blue link next to the yellow stars that says, "customer reviews."

As always...
It's a great day to be alive!

Get/Share Your FREE SSD Mental Health Chronicles at www.senseiselfdevelopment.care

Sensei Self Development

FOR ADULTS

An Introduction to Mindfulness

Sensei Paul David

Check Out The SSD Chronicles Series [CLICK HERE](#)
Set As Browser Favorite

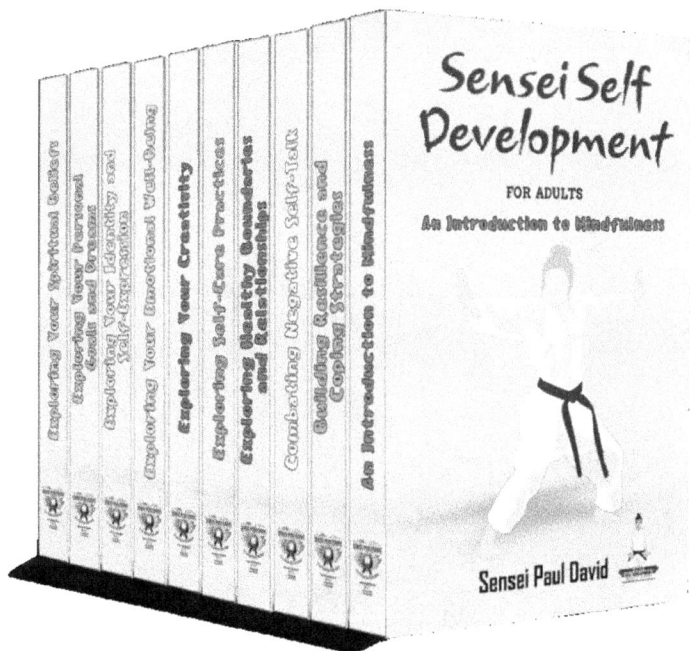

Get/Share Your FREE All-Ages Mental Health eBook Now at

www.senseiselfdevelopment.com

Or CLICK HERE

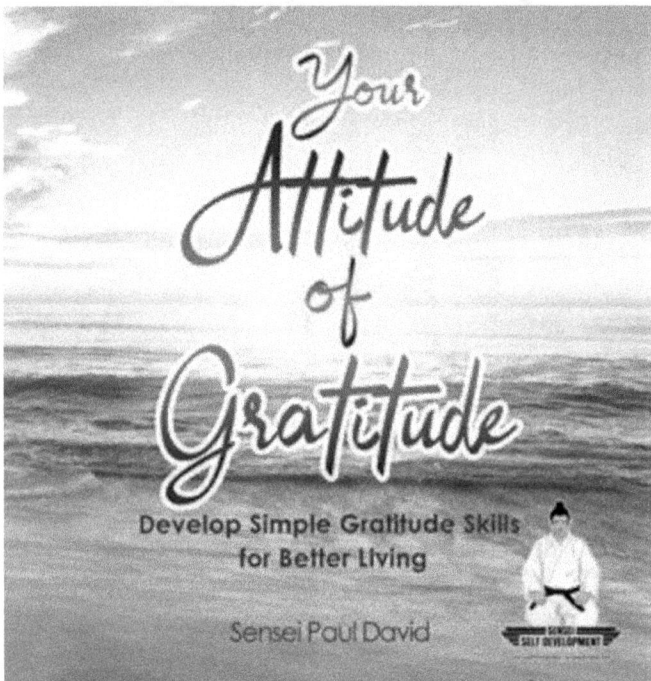

senseiselfdevelopment.com

Click Another Book In The
SSD BOOK SERIES:
senseipublishing.com/SSD_SERIES
CLICK HERE

SENSEI
SELF DEVELOPMENT
BOOKS SERIES
senseiselfdevelopment.senseipublishing.com

Get/Share Our FREE All-Ages Mental Health Books Now!

FREE Kids Books

FREE Self-Development Book for Every Family

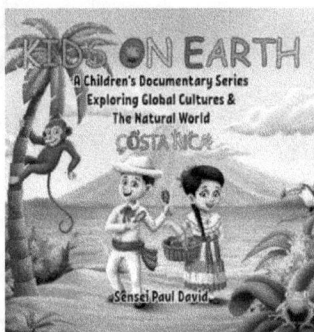

Click Below or Search Amazon for Another Book In Each Series Or Visit:

www.senseipublishing.com/CompleteLibrary

KIDS ON EARTH

kidsonearth.senseipublishing.com

life of Bailey

lifeofbailey.senseipublishing.com

SENSEI SELF DEVELOPMENT

BOOKS SERIES

senseiselfdevelopment.senseipublishing.com

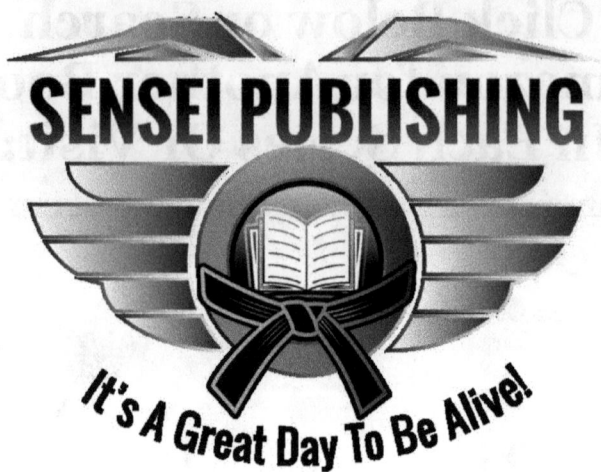

Join Our Publishing Journey!

If you would like to receive FREE BOOKS, special offers, please visit www.senseipublishing.com and join our newsletter by entering your email address in the pop-up box

Get Our FREE Books Today!

Click & Share the Links Below

FREE Kids Books

lifeofbailey.senseipublishing.com
kidsonearth.senseipublishing.com

FREE Self-Development Book

senseiselfdevelopment.senseipublishing.com

Join Our Publishing Journey!

If you would like to receive FREE BOOKS, please visit **www.senseipublishing.com**. Join our newsletter by entering your email address in the pop-up box

Follow Sensei Paul David on Amazon
CLICK THE LOGO BELOW

FREE BONUS!!!
Experience Over 25 FREE Engaging Guided Meditations!

Prized Skills & Practices for Adults & Kids. Help Restore sleep, Lower Stress, Improve Posture, Navigate Uncertainty and more.

Download the Free Insight Timer App and click the link below:
http://insig.ht/sensei_paul

About Sensei Publishing

Sensei Publishing commits itself to helping people of all ages transform into better versions of themselves by providing high-quality and research-based self-development books with an emphasis on mental health and guided meditations. Sensei Publishing offers well-written e-books, audiobooks, paperbacks, and online courses that simplify complicated but practical topics in line with its mission to inspire people toward positive transformation.

It's a great day to be alive!

About the Author

I create simple & transformative eBooks and guided Meditations for Adults and children proven to help navigate uncertainty, solve niche problems & bring families closer together.

I'm a former finance project manager, private pilot, jiu-jitsu instructor, musician & former University of Toronto Fitness Trainer. I prefer a science-based approach to focus on these & other areas in my life to stay humble & hungry to evolve. I hope you enjoy my work and I'd love to hear your feedback.

- It's a great day to be alive!
Sensei Paul David

Scan & Follow/Like/Subscribe: Facebook, Instagram, YouTube: @senseipublishing

Scan using your phone/iPad camera for Social Media Visit us at www.senseipublishing.com and sign up for our newsletter to learn more about our exciting books and to experience our FREE Guided Meditations for Kids and adults.

www.ingramcontent.com/pod-product-compliance
Lightning Source LLC
Chambersburg PA
CBHW051711020426
42333CB00014B/938